this book
belongs to:

authors

Hugh Halter & Matt Smay

purpose

After we wrote *The Tangible Kingdom*, we were besieged with letters from people wondering how to put these ideas into practice in their own lives and churches. At the same time, we were facing new challenges in our own community that made us wish we had a way of helping larger numbers of people through the same process that we ourselves had been through. Thus, the idea of *The Tangible Kingdom Primer* came to be. And now here it is. We hope it helps you.

book design & layout

Peter Schrock

technical assistance from Kevin Tracy at kevintracydesign.com

editors

Peter Schrock, Celine Baldemor, Lily Chou

Special thanks to Caesar Kalinowski, Jeff Vanderstelt and Soma Communities for their editing contributions.

copyrights

published by

Missio Publishing

thanks

Matt & Hugh wish to thank Church Resource Ministries for their commitment to Missio and their investment and help in publishing the first edition of this resource for the Church worldwide. Most notably, we thank Peter Schrock for his creative vision and design. We also thank the people of Adullam for living this out in real life.

for more info or to find out about bulk discounts

tangiblekingdom.com

missio.us

ISBN 978-0-9823233-0-4 (revision 3)

Printed in China

an eight-week guide to incarnational community

THE
TANGIBLE
KINGDOM
primer

TABLE OF CONTENTS

The Tangible Kingdom Primer:
HOW TO USE THIS BOOK

Have you ever watched someone who "made it look easy?" Someone who does something difficult without seeming to put out any effort? Maybe a talented performer, a great speaker, a gifted cook, or artist. Like seeing Tiger Woods hit a golf ball, Beyoncé sing, or Al Pacino play the gangster? They make it look so natural, don't they? Part of our amazement often comes from the fact that we've have tried to do the same thing only to realize how difficult it really is.

Why the difference? Well, there are many reasons. Some people are naturally gifted in certain areas. But one foundational issue stands out: *making it look easy takes a lot of practice.*

So it is with incarnational life and missional community.

Everyone's talking about community. Everyone seems to want it, most complain if they don't find it, but it's harder to pull off than you'd think. People complain of time constraints, busyness, fear, and often have memories of community gone bad. We've got children to deal with. Some people struggle to relate well socially. We're often 30 minutes drive or more away from people we like to hang out with. We're stressed about money. We overwork, and when we do get some free time, we have a hard time sharing that time with others. Sure, we all know we need this thing called "community" and we even have some inklings that tell us that our friends need it too. Yet, a Grand Canyon-sized gap exists between our hopes and our realities.

So what's the problem? What do we do? And will it be worth it?

Nothing good ever comes easy. For sure, nothing of God's Kingdom comes without resistance from our personal kingdoms or the world's kingdom. Nothing of the Spirit of God comes without a good ol' fashioned bar fight from our flesh. Galatians 5 reminds us, "So I say live by the Spirit, and you will not gratify the desires of the sinful nature. For the sinful nature desires what is contrary to the Spirit, and the Spirit what is contrary to the sinful nature. They are in conflict with each other, so that you do not do what you want."

It sounds pretty basic, but it's true. The reason we struggle to live a missional life is that it pulls against every natural fiber, sin, rhythm, habit, muscle, and thought pattern we're used to.

As we said in *The Tangible Kingdom*, God's ways are natural, but they aren't easy—especially at first. New ways of life must be formed in us through hours, days, and years of intentional practice. The future of your own faith and the incarnational presence of your community is ultimately about letting the Spirit of God re-orient everything about you.

This is why we've called this resource a "primer" (which can be defined as *a book of elementary principles*). While we know a workbook alone won't get the job done, we do think it can provide a good place to start. God's Kingdom doesn't usually unfold in a nice, neat package or linear progression. In fact, he is much more likely to surprise us, to show up in unexpected places and in unique experiences that only he can orchestrate. Our hope for this book is that it will help you to be ready when he does. This includes listening and being willing to be changed. It also includes learning to take personal responsibility for your own calling and dealing with those parts of your flesh that keep you from following Jesus as he leads you out into the world.

With all this in mind, we've written this primer with two specific purposes. First, to be *a spiritual formation tool* to prepare your heart for mission. We definitely want you to grab some friends to go through this with, but you don't have to commit to being an incarnational community yet. You can just be "friends who are going through an eight-week spiritual formation exercise together." You can hold each other accountable, you'll actually get to be missional together, and you'll have a much better experience by processing the struggles together. While some of the specifics of the study may seem premature if you're in a non-committal setting, we suggest that you use the opportunity to get acquainted with the ideas and consider their meaning for your life.

The second purpose for the primer is to be *a field guide for starting mission together*. Some of you are ready to go and have friends that can't wait to begin. If that's you, then dive right in to the spiritual exercises as both heart formation and missional practice.

In either case, at the end of the eight weeks, you'll have the opportunity to decide what you're going to do next. Remember, this is just a primer for building lifelong habits. Some of you will just thank each other and move on; others will decide to formalize your commitment to go on mission together; and the field-guide people can just keep rolling along. There's no failure here, just a chance to engage at the pace that you're ready for.

The Tangible Kingdom Primer:
NOT JUST ABOUT EVANGELISM

You might have noticed...people don't like to be "evangelized." They don't automatically think our truths are their truths. They won't show up at our church gatherings to hear our ideas and they can't stand it when we push them to accept our concepts. Yet one truth always remains, people will always be drawn to good news when they see it in action. Though they may not understand everything, the Gospel...is always Good News when it touches down in real life.

The Tangible Kingdom Primer is about learning how to live in the Kingdom and how to create pathways for others to experience it along with you. Yes, we believe that many of your friends will find God along the way and that evangelism will happen, but this process is really about discipleship. Becoming an apprentice of Christ is the goal. So as you begin, focus on your own spiritual formation, and leave the results to God. This is not a guide to "saving souls." It's an invitation to enlarge your entire spiritual formation process.

The Tangible Kingdom Primer:
BEFORE YOU BEGIN

Hopefully, you've had a chance to get familiar with the posture and practices of incarnational community by reading *The Tangible Kingdom* book. Although the book gives a broader background of the key concepts, this primer is designed as a stand-alone resource. If you are new to faith in Jesus, it will help move you into mission regardless of whether you know a lot of details, history, or theology. If your group is full of people who have been Christians for a long time, the primer will provide a basis for getting beyond the typical "comsumer" church experience. So for all community leaders, and most participants, we still recommend beginning with *The Tangible Kingdom* book. It's a key resource as you develop your missional community. But don't let that stop you if you're ready to get going!

As we begin, we'll first provide a quick summary of some key concepts that you will need to understand in order to get everyone in your community on the same page. We'd also like to share a few thoughts that will help you move beyond "just another small group experience." Our intent is to provide a new framework for how you can live both naturally and intentionally to make the Gospel of God's Kingdom tangible to you and anyone you love.

We hope that after finishing the eight-week guide, the new habits of incarnational community have become so ingrained in your heart and behavior that the activities become intuitive instead of regimented. Most small group guides assume that by completing the assignments you will accomplish the end goal of establishing a community or small group. Our viewpoint is a little different. We hope that at the end of the eight weeks, you will have successfully begun the journey of fostering the posture and practices of an incarnational community. So, the end is just the beginning! Keep this in mind as you wrestle through each week and adjust your expectations accordingly.

The Tangible Kingdom Primer:
BASIC CONCEPTS

We'll define many of these ideas further as we go through the study, but here are some of the concepts that you can expect to run into...

Gospel: the good news of Jesus, capable of transforming everything about a person, their community, and their world.

Missional People: individuals actively committed to living a "sent" life in the context of community.

Sojourner: a spiritually disoriented God seeker who is interacting with the missional community.

Incarnational Community: a group of people with the posture, tone, motives, and heart of Jesus; those who physically represent him in a particular location.

Posture: the attitude of the body; the way a person or community expresses itself to others, especially in nonverbal ways.

Apprenticeship: moving beyond knowledge-based discipleship to action-oriented followership, with the goal of living like Jesus lived. This comes through regular practice, faith-oriented action, and personal devotion to know the ways of Christ.

Living Out: the natural and deliberate process of living among, listening to, and loving people in culture with the the desire to connect them to the Christian community.

Inviting In: integrating sojourners into the community as a result of living out the Gospel with intentional hospitality and compassion.

The Intuitive Life: our choices, motives, decisions now led by the Holy Spirit. A Spirit-empowered lifestyle guided by a capacity to sense and respond to God's direction.

The Tangible Kingdom Primer:
THE WEEKLY RHYTHM

Incarnational community is the framework of life in which God has called us all to live. It's the best context for our spiritual growth. It will provide the most natural way to enlarge the Gospel picture for your friends who are seeking God right now. But as we said, it doesn't just happen on its own.

So we're going to provide an initial pathway that will help you and your community deal with the inner-life challenges to mission, as well as some intentional activities and reflections that we have found helpful for us. To do this you'll notice that the primer is set up in a daily format for each person to complete individually.

We suggest planning to spend about 20 minutes a day on this. As with any spiritual formation practice, we highly recommend you take those 20 minutes seriously. Take time to get in a quiet, undistracted space, breathe, begin with silence, then invite God to speak. Read every word slowly and fight the urge to move too quickly. Every question has a purpose. Every scripture is the breath of God. If you ask God to direct your thoughts and writing, HE WILL. If you just buzz through it, you'll miss him.

Day 5 of the sequence is designed to be done together with a group of people. After all, one of our main values is community!

Although we're following what appears to be a highly structured process, we all know that life doesn't always work like this. Our hope is that the structure we're creating of seven daily practices and reflections will help you begin to understand and incorporate into life the key components to personal and communal renewal.

DAY 1: EXPLORATION

The first day of the weekly rhythm will introduce you to the subject of the week and provide thoughts, stories, and definitions to help you begin to get an understanding of the concepts.

We'll also provide questions and journaling space so that you can wrestle with what this stuff means in your own life and in the life of your community. And here's fair warning: we've intentionally written questions that we hope will challenge you. They may even make you uncomfortable sometimes. We look at it this way: we can make these eight weeks easy and somewhat pointless, or we can give room for the Gospel to get in deep where it can make a difference. The good news is that if you let it, it will change your life. And that is what we're after.

DAY 2: MEDITATION

On Day 2, we'll provide you with a scripture or two to soak in for a little while. Read it a couple times and let it do its work in you. Don't forget the questions on the next page.

DAY 3: CHANGE

The Change Day is where we start to get serious. What does this idea mean in your life? How would your life be different if you began to let it be changed by the Gospel? There are questions for journaling on this day as well.

DAY 4: ACTION

So by now you've begun to let your heart be changed. Now how about your feet? Action Day is about putting it into practice. As we work our way through these eight weeks, we'll give you ideas each week for taking action.

DAY 5: COMMUNITY

Just when you're needing a little encouragement, Community Day comes along. This is the day when you get together with the other members of your community (those other folks who are putting this stuff into practice along with you).

In our opinion, this is the most important day of the week. In fact, we'll let you in on a secret: this whole process is going to be really difficult to pull off unless you do it with a few friends. Healthy relationships (with God and with each other) are at the center of all that we're talking about. Besides, the fondue night in Week 6 will be much more fun with friends sharing the food.

DAY 6: CALIBRATION

On Day 6, we'll revisit the theme of the week from a different angle and give you some additional things to think about as you allow God to bring transformation to your life.

DAY 7: ReCREATE

The last day of the cycle is a rest day or a sabbath. We challenge you to use this day in ways that are intentionally restful. In other words, hang out with friends or family. Don't multitask. Don't over schedule. This day should help recalibrate the biblical pattern we like to call ReCreate: we **rest** in Jesus' completed work on our behalf, and out of that rest we **create** value, beauty, and good works.

Set aside time on your sabbath day for listening. We tend to keep so busy that we couldn't hear God if he were shouting at us. And he rarely shouts. Stop for a little while and listen.

The Tangible Kingdom Primer:
PUTTING A GROUP TOGETHER

We have learned that it helps to give people time to process the tough inner life issues individually and then come together as a community to share and experience a new reality together. Before you begin the process, pick a day your community will initially begin to meet. Ultimately the goal is to increasingly begin to live like a family on God's mission together throughout the week. What starts out as a weekly meeting will grow into a lifestyle.

As we've already mentioned, we suggest you find a group of people who will do this with you. You can present the idea to a group you're already a part of, like a house church or bible study group. Or you can invite some friends to join you in creating a new community. In either case, there doesn't have to be any initial commitment beyond getting together weekly to explore these ideas together.

While there are no limitations on the number of people in your initial community, we have found that somewhere in the 4-12 range is usually preferred. Typically, a group this size can easily fit in most homes, is large enough to accommodate the occasional absentee, and is small enough not to require a coordinator to facilitate meals together. The group can include mature believers, new Christ followers, and sojourners that may not be sure about their beliefs.

Remember the actual mission Jesus sends his followers on is a disciple-making mission. These communities are ultimately going to be about helping yourself and others increasingly walk in Jesus' ways as you apply the Gospel to every area of your life.

Use the space provided on the next page to write down the details for your first community time.

Write the names of people that you want to invite and plan a time to get them together to start the journey. Aim for 4 to 12 participants.

What day will your community initially meet each week?

Where will you get together for the first meeting? Maybe a home, cafe, or park?

What day will everyone need to start the primer (-4 days from the first meeting)?

WHAT IS MISSIONAL?

As we get started, we want to begin with a word that sets the stage for our journey together. The word is *missional*. Like many words, it can mean a lot of things depending on your background. For our work together, we'll remind you that it essentially means "sent."

Most Christians would agree that there is a basic call on every believer's life to live missionally. The Old Testament uses words like "sojourners" or "wanderers" as precursors to New Testament words like "aliens, foreigners, strangers, or ambassadors." All these words represent the reality that a Christian's life is transitory. In simple language, it means that we are passing through this life with a sense of purpose, duty, passion, and responsibility for the "mission of God." We are a "sent" people because of the work of the Gospel and the trajectory it produces in our lives. (More on that later.)

A missional life is a gospel-centered life. However, for the vast majority of Christians the challenge to discover and faithfully live out a missional call that is truly centered around the Gospel can be confusing and often frustrating.

After coaching hundreds of leaders, we've come to realize that times of despair, doubt, frustration, and personal letdown are as much a part of God's work in our lives as anything else. When challenged by financial distress, health issues, broken relationships, or general emotional melancholy, we tend to get much more serious— even desperate—about hearing from God. During these times, we recognize our human frailty and limited control over our circumstances. When we allow God to work in our lives, our latent missional call begins to come alive.

The foundation of a missional life is the decision to offer to God our plans in exchange for his plans. It is to allow the truth about who God is, what he has done, and our new identity in Jesus inform all of life. It requires that we are willing to leave our world so he can send us to extend his Kingdom. Whether we choose to engage the call is up to us.

What is missional?

THE FOUNDATION OF A MISSIONAL LIFE IS THE DECISION TO OFFER TO GOD OUR PLANS IN EXCHANGE FOR HIS PLANS.

Sent

A TURNING POINT (MATT)

As a college student, I had very little interest in anything ministry related. In fact, from the age of 12 my dream was to play college baseball, become an engineer, and expand the family contracting business. I was well on my way to realizing this dream; I had made the team at a Division I school and was in my junior year of an engineering program.

That's when the dream completely unraveled. I'll spare you the details, but in the midst of a broken engagement, I took a small step toward God for some much needed help.

What happened next was a two-year journey that concluded with a decision to give up a chance at a professional baseball career and, instead, move to Oregon to pursue a biblical education.

For someone that grew up in church, despised youth groups, and swore he'd never be a pastor, this was a dramatic change in plans.

List a few of the difficult times in your life. How did you view God? Did you doubt him? Question his leading? Take matters into your own hands?

Look over the experiences you've listed. What do you think God was doing with you during these times?

What things have you had to give up to follow God?

Right now, is there anything hindering you from making the decision to live a missional life?

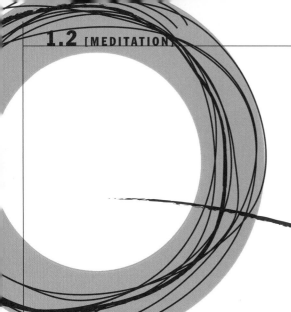

In *The Tangible Kingdom*, we walked you through the first biblical story of intentional missionality. Abraham was called by God to leave his homeland, much of his family, and most of the comforts of home in order to go to a pagan country.

THE LORD HAD SAID TO ABRAHAM, "LEAVE YOUR COUNTRY, YOUR PEOPLE AND YOUR FATHER'S HOUSEHOLD AND GO TO THE LAND I WILL SHOW YOU."

"I WILL MAKE YOU INTO A GREAT NATION AND I WILL BLESS YOU. I WILL MAKE YOUR NAME GREAT, AND YOU WILL BE A BLESSING."

SO ABRAHAM LEFT, AS THE LORD HAD TOLD HIM AND LOT WENT WITH HIM. ABRAHAM WAS SEVENTY-FIVE YEARS OLD WHEN HE SET OUT FROM HARAN.

HE TOOK HIS WIFE SARAI, HIS NEPHEW LOT, ALL THE POSSESSIONS THEY HAD ACCUMULATED AND THE PEOPLE THEY HAD ACQUIRED IN HARAN, AND THEY SET OUT FOR THE LAND OF CANAAN.

- FROM GENESIS 12

Abraham wasn't given many of the specifics. In fact, all he was told was that the blessing God was giving him would extend through him to the whole world.

Throughout the scriptures, we see God calling his followers to live a life of "sentness." Stability, social comfort, relational control, safety, success, respect, or clarity were not expected. People had to go purely out of obedience, a personal sense of calling, in faith, and simply because they loved God. Outcome didn't matter; faithfulness did.

Jesus asked his disciples to leave their nets while still clueless. As they walked and lived with him, they learned that his ways challenged their ways. In fact, his plans would often pull them into the unknown and into situations that forced them to trust the miraculous.

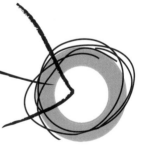

People who wanted to follow without adjusting their lives were often repelled by his honesty. "The Son of Man has no place to lay his head," he told the teacher of the law.

The night Jesus ate with his disciples, he gave them the clear sense that after he left they'd be wandering the world, despised and on the run, led only by the Holy Spirit. In each of the letters from Paul we observe the early faith communities facing many tensions related to being sent.

There's no way to say it gently: *spreading God's blessing to the world does not come easy.*

Christian people are a people on the move, constantly sent by God to the world. To be missional is the call of every church. It's the call of every Christian. Jesus said to his followers, to us, "As the Father has sent me, I am sending you."

Abraham's Big Choice

Go	Stay
Sacrifice	Safety
Blessing	Comfort
Risk	Stability
Hope	Security
Adventure	Status Quo
Fear	Boredom
Change	Control
Faith	Expectations

As you ponder those words above, put yourself in the shoes of Abraham's community or in the faith communities just after Jesus died.

What emotions might they have felt when they heard this call to GO?

What is missional?

Which words on the lists do you value the most?

As you consider your call to GO, what emotions are you feeling?

What challenges get in the way of you going?

for m
thought
are not you
thoughts

As Abraham is sent, as the early Christian communities were sent, we notice Four Immersions they experienced...

they were immersed in a new culture.

Abraham headed into a hostile culture that didn't care for his God. Peter and the early Jewish communities were called into Gentile and Greek cultures through the leadership of Paul. The great missionary movements throughout our history have been called to cross ethnic, social, religious, and philosophical barriers to extend God's blessing. They had to live with people that didn't respect their God or eat their food. They didn't have much control over how these cultures might impact their lives and they had to trust God to be with them in these foreign environments.

they were immersed in community.

You'll notice they never lived out their sentness alone. Abraham took a small band with him. Jesus gathered a small band to himself and whenever he sent them out, it was at least two by two. The stories of our early monastic or denominational movements almost always had small communities at their core.

1

they were immersed
in god.

God didn't call Abraham or the early communities to be evangelistic, share four laws, or hand out tracts. He told them to bless the world with the blessing God gave them. Blessing means "the tangible touch of God." To share a program or a book or a principle doesn't require you to know God. But to give the blessing of God to people you must be immersed in him. Jesus said it this way: "Apart from me you can do nothing."

they were immersed
in tension.

It should be clear by now that being sent sometimes includes living with some internal and social tension. The early communities had to get used to walking by faith as they sought God's guidance on a daily basis. They didn't have pastors to give them a program to follow. They didn't have books to train them or websites with cool resources. People thought they were nuts. They had little or no financial backing, travel was slow, and the language barriers were widespread. Every day was a new journey.

neither are your
ways my ways,
declares the lord

Think through the Four Immersions -- culture, community, God, tension. Which ones might have been the most difficult for Abraham?

Which ones do you personally find the most intimidating? Why?

Write down examples in your life of each of the Four Immersions.

What are your hopes as you apply the Four Immersions?

Imagine if Jesus were to walk into the room you're in right now and say, "Come on, get up, and come with me."

Where do you picture him taking you first? Maybe it's someone's home. If so, whose? Maybe it's someplace you've never been. Where? Why would he take you there?

This week we'd like you to practice "sentness" by crossing three barriers of normal life:

cross your fence.

Do something to bless or simply converse with one neighbor on your street.

cross your street.

Do something to connect with someone who is close to your home, but with whom you haven't built a relationship yet.

cross a social, political, or ethnic barrier.

Take someone with you from your missional community. Consider these ideas: eat at an authentically ethnic restaurant in a part of town that is unfamiliar to you, attend a lecture or event that represents a different part of culture, visit a church or other religious location with different beliefs than your own.

As you meet for the first time as a community, here are some things to do:

>> Exchange contact information to make it easier for your community to stay connected.

COMMUNITY MEMBERS/MISSIONAL PEOPLE
[individuals actively committed to living a "sent" life in the context of community]

Name   Phone Number   Email Address

>> Take some time individually to make a list of all the sojourners you know who you might want to include in your community. Share it with the group.

SOJOURNERS
[spiritually curious God-seeking travelers who have intersected the missional community]

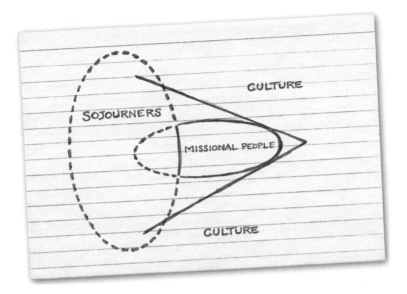

1

Questions for group discussion:

What's something about yourself that the people in the group don't know?

What are two lifelong dreams of yours? Name one you've accomplished and one you haven't.

Pray together for the sojourners you have listed.

NEXT WEEK...

Meet at a group member's home or some other place where you can share a meal together.

The New Testament is full of wild stories that encourage us to live differently. One word, however, stands as a clarion call to God's work of transformation in the world. The word is "Go." It may take some adjustment on our part to realize this, but nothing of God's Kingdom happens unless someone is willing to GO.

WE ARE A FAMILY OF
MISSIONARY SERVANTS
SENT TO SERVE THE WORLD
AND MAKE DISCIPLES OF JESUS.

Sometimes GOING will require a 30-second email to encourage a friend, a five-minute walk across the street to help a neighbor, or the willingness to give up a quiet evening with your spouse in exchange for inviting some friends over who don't know Christ. Other times, GOING may require a week-long commitment, a large chunk of money, or even a lifelong commitment to leave your city or country to serve God.

Whatever the case, the word GO will cost you something. It will require that you creatively look for the opportunities that God provides you to leave what's natural and self-serving in order to extend his love to others.

What is missional?

SAYING 'YES'

Our family has committed to do our best never to turn down an invite to spend time with either our community, neighbors, or sojourning friends.

We've found this makes a dramatic difference in the way people perceive our commitment to being in relationship with them. It only takes a few times of saying "no" before people will stop inviting you because they think you're not interested.

TITHING YOUR TIME

In a normal week, we eat around 21 meals, give or take a few. One of the ways we've challenged our own community to be missional is to ask them to commit to sharing one of those meals with sojourners.

Or another way to think about it is to do a quick analysis of how much time we spend watching TV, surfing the internet, or reading. Can we give 10% of that time to be with or help another person?

Think of the family members, friends, neighbors, and co-workers among whom God might be sending you to incarnate the Gospel. As you think of them, consider the following...

What do you think it would take for them to connect with your community in the future?

How much time per week are you willing to give to building deeper relationships with them?

What tangible needs do they have that could be opportunities for you to be good news to them?

What activities or hobbies do you love to do that you could invite them to share with you?

HE IS WOOING YOU FROM THE JAWS OF DISTRESS TO A SPACIOUS PLACE FREE FROM RESTRICTION, TO THE COMFORT OF YOUR TABLE LADEN WITH CHOICE FOOD. JOB 36:16

YOU PREPARE A TABLE BEFORE ME IN THE PRESENCE OF MY ENEMIES. YOU ANOINT MY HEAD WITH OIL; MY CUP OVERFLOWS.

SURELY GOODNESS AND LOVE WILL FOLLOW ME ALL THE DAYS OF MY LIFE, AND I WILL DWELL IN THE HOUSE OF THE LORD FOREVER. PSALM 23:5-6

FOR WHO IS GREATER, THE ONE WHO IS AT THE TABLE OR THE ONE WHO SERVES? IS IT NOT THE ONE WHO IS AT THE TABLE? BUT I AM AMONG YOU AS ONE WHO SERVES. LUKE 22:27

What is missional?

THEN JESUS SAID TO HIS HOST, "WHEN YOU GIVE A LUNCHEON OR DINNER, DO NOT INVITE YOUR FRIENDS, YOUR BROTHERS OR RELATIVES, OR YOUR RICH NEIGHBORS; IF YOU DO, THEY MAY INVITE YOU BACK AND SO YOU WILL BE REPAID. BUT WHEN YOU GIVE A BANQUET, INVITE THE POOR, THE CRIPPLED, THE LAME, THE BLIND, AND YOU WILL BE BLESSED. ALTHOUGH THEY CANNOT REPAY YOU, YOU WILL BE REPAID AT THE RESURRECTION OF THE RIGHTEOUS."

WHEN ONE OF THOSE AT THE TABLE WITH HIM HEARD THIS, HE SAID TO JESUS, "BLESSED IS THE MAN WHO WILL EAT AT THE FEAST IN THE KINGDOM OF GOD." JESUS REPLIED: "A CERTAIN MAN WAS PREPARING A GREAT BANQUET AND INVITED MANY GUESTS. AT THE TIME OF THE BANQUET HE SENT HIS SERVANT TO TELL THOSE WHO HAD BEEN INVITED, 'COME, FOR EVERYTHING IS NOW READY.' BUT THEY ALL ALIKE BEGAN TO MAKE EXCUSES.

THE FIRST SAID, 'I HAVE JUST BOUGHT A FIELD, AND I MUST GO AND SEE IT. PLEASE EXCUSE ME.' ANOTHER SAID, 'I HAVE JUST BOUGHT FIVE YOKE OF OXEN, AND I'M ON MY WAY TO TRY THEM OUT. PLEASE EXCUSE ME.' STILL ANOTHER SAID, 'I JUST GOT MARRIED, SO I CAN'T COME.'

THE SERVANT CAME BACK AND REPORTED THIS TO HIS MASTER. THEN THE OWNER OF THE HOUSE BECAME ANGRY AND ORDERED HIS SERVANT, 'GO OUT QUICKLY INTO THE STREETS AND ALLEYS OF THE TOWN AND BRING IN THE POOR, THE CRIPPLED, THE BLIND AND THE LAME.' 'SIR,' THE SERVANT SAID, 'WHAT YOU ORDERED HAS BEEN DONE, BUT THERE IS STILL ROOM.'

THEN THE MASTER TOLD HIS SERVANT, 'GO OUT TO THE ROADS AND COUNTRY LANES AND MAKE THEM COME IN, SO THAT MY HOUSE WILL BE FULL. I TELL YOU, NOT ONE OF THOSE MEN WHO WERE INVITED WILL GET A TASTE OF MY BANQUET.' LUKE 14

1

As we saw on Day 2 of this week, being missional has two components. On one hand, we receive blessing from God. On the other, we pass it on to others. We receive in abundance from the table of God's provision and grace not for us to hoard away, but rather to carry into the world. Therefore, sharing a meal is both a reminder of God's amazing provision for our needs through Jesus, but it is also a powerful and living display of the Gospel. Eating meals together becomes integral to the mission.

WHAT IS INCARNATIONAL?

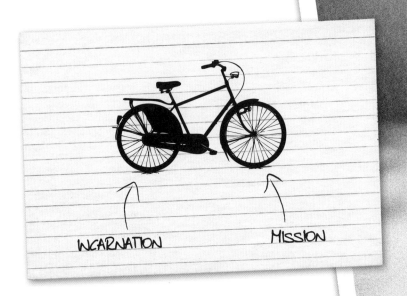

INCARNATION   MISSION

So far we've learned that mission is the "sending" impulse and call for every Christian. Amazingly, however, that impulse can send people off into really goofy or offensive behavior in the world. For the sake of "mission" some people threaten abortion clinics or preach fire and brimstone with a megaphone on a street corner, trying to start spiritual conversations with people with whom they have no relationship.

Paul described his ministry this way: "We loved you so much that we were delighted to share with you not only the gospel of God but our lives as well, because you had become so dear to us. Surely you remember, brothers, our toil and hardship, we worked night and day in order not to be a burden to anyone while we preached the gospel of God to you." [1 Thessalonians 2:8-9]

Like harsh words spoken without tact, or a fire burning outside a fireplace, missionality by itself can hurt the cause of Christ more than it helps. This is why *missional* has an inseparable twin. The word is *incarnational*. It means "to take on flesh." If missional means "to go," incarnation is about *how* you go and what people see as you go. It encompasses your posture, your tone, your motives, and your heart. Incarnation is critical because it will eventually determine whether or not people will want to know you or your God.

What is incarnational?

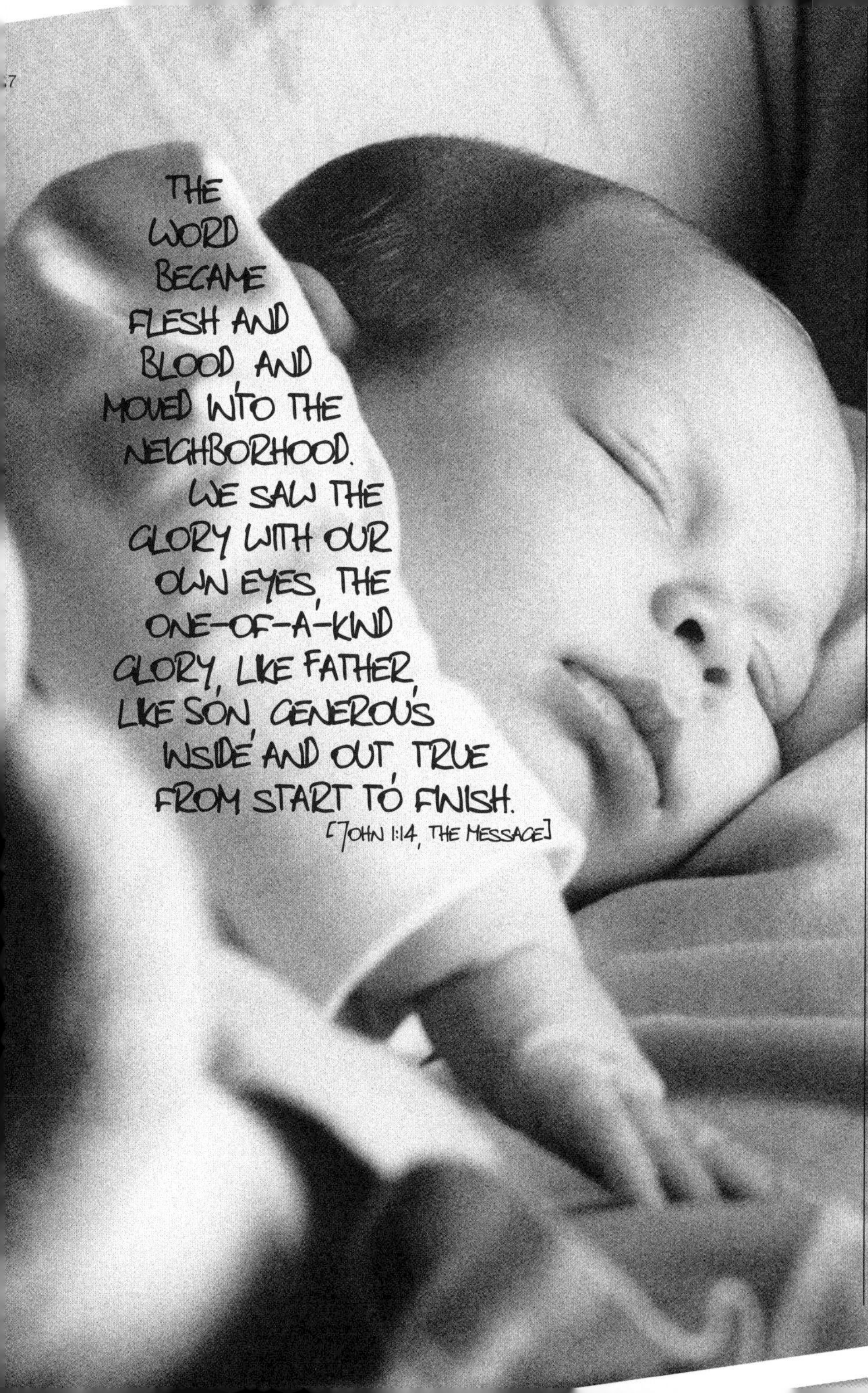

THE
WORD
BECAME
FLESH AND
BLOOD, AND
MOVED INTO THE
NEIGHBORHOOD.
WE SAW THE
GLORY WITH OUR
OWN EYES, THE
ONE-OF-A-KIND
GLORY, LIKE FATHER,
LIKE SON, GENEROUS
INSIDE AND OUT, TRUE
FROM START TO FINISH.
[JOHN 1:14, THE MESSAGE]

2

What do think about these slogans? What kind of posture do they represent?

What do you think about Jesus being viewed as a friend of sinners?

What does that tell us about his posture?

What do you think Jesus was like for the first 30 years before his ministry?

In Acts 3:1-7, there is a great story of Peter and John heading to the temple to pray. On their way, they ran into a lame man who was begging for money. Peter and John ministered to this man out on the street and it resulted in a great spiritual awakening with many would-be Christ-followers.

Have you ever taken the time to recognize how many times God shows up "on the way"? That is, as an interruption to our normal schedules? Peter and John were following a ritual of heading to the church to pray, meet with God, and be with other devout Jews. As an interruption to their expected walk, they ran into a setup by God.

It's interesting how so many people have come to expect God to show up during our "spiritual times." You know, during the sermon, the prayer time, the Bible study, or the worship service. That's where he heals us, teaches us, speaks to us, comforts us, or guides us...at least that's what we think.

Yet, the scriptures give us a very different picture. People got healed out on the streets. Non-Christians saw the power of the early communities and encountered Christ around tables, while sitting on a hill listening to him teach, walking with him on a road, standing on a shore, or while getting some water at a well. Many of the most powerful stories happened "along the way." In most cases, Jesus and the people that followed him met others in the context of their normal lives. God showed up in the middle of real life.

Incarnation speaks to our posture, our timing, and how much of our time we give people before we ever share biblical truths with them. But incarnation also speaks to where the most important times of ministry will take place. To be incarnational, therefore, means that we must begin where Jesus began with us: OUT THERE! WITH PEOPLE! ALONG THE WAY!

What is incarnational?

one day peter and john were
going up to the temple at
the time of prayer at three in
the afternoon. now a man
crippled from birth was being
carried to the temple gate
called beautiful, where he
was put every day to beg from
those going into the temple
courts. when he saw peter
and john about to enter, he
asked them for money. peter
looked straight at him, as did
john. then peter said, look at
us! so the man gave them
his attention, expecting to
get something from them.
then peter said, silver or gold
i do not have, but what i
have i give you. in the name
of jesus christ of nazareth,
walk. taking him by the right
hand, he helped him up, and
instantly the man's feet and
ankles became strong.

(acts 3:1-7)

Below is a list of scripture references from the Gospels of Luke
and John. Read through them and write down the environment for
some of Jesus' "along the way" moments.

Reference	Event	Where it happened
John 2.1-10	Turned water into wine	
John 3.1-4	Talked after hours with Nicodemus	
John 4.4-10	Met Samaritan social outcast	
Luke 4.38-44	Healed mother-in-law	
Luke 5.1-8	Called the disciples	
Luke 5.17-26	Healed the paralytic	
Luke 7.11-19	Raised man from dead	
Luke 9.10-11	Fed the 5000	
Luke 17.11-19	Healed the lepers	

What is incarnational?

What is significant about the context (place, environment, type of people) in each of these biblical events?

2

"NEITHER DO I CONDEMN YOU," JESUS DECLARED. "GO NOW AND LEAVE YOUR LIFE OF SIN."

What is incarnational?

In John 8, we find a powerful story of a woman who was caught in adultery. The religious guys were using her sin to try to test Jesus' commitment to judge sinners. According to Old Testament law, Jesus was expected to condone her death by stoning. But Jesus didn't. Instead he became her advocate, protected her, and turned the question of judgment back to the religious people.

This small but revolutionary act set Jesus apart, not only from the expectations of the people of his time, but also from what you and I would generally expect. Judgment still exists inside the church toward people who sin. Sinners expect Christians to judge their behavior. All too often, we do.

The definition of an advocate is one who looks past the outward behavior, vices, sin, frailty, brokenness, and confusion of a person. Instead an advocate focuses on winning a person's trust, friendship, and loyalty. When those things are established, the heart and desire to obey God come naturally.

This is why we must change our POSTURE. Our posture is what wins a person's respect and heart and helps them be open to God's ways. While poor posture communicates judgment, Christ-like posture displays love.

2

Why do you think Jesus chose to get involved in the woman's story?

How is an advocate different than a friend?

What does it require of us to become advocates?

What is the risk for us in advocating for sinners?

What is incarnational?

Why is it hard to advocate for people that struggle
with obvious sin?

2

Who have you been an advocate for?

Who in your life needs you to be an advocate for them now?

Spend some time today in a shopping mall, a downtown café, or a coffee shop that overlooks a busy crosswalk, a popular park, or a college campus area.

Simply sit still and look at the faces that go past you. Imagine some of the things that might make up their life stories: sadness, abuse, abandonment, broken relationships, sexual mistakes, unemployment fears, lack of purpose, broken marriages, deep debt, bankruptcy, loneliness, despair, pressure to measure up, desire for community, searching for God, parents who haven't understood or cared for their children well. Pray for them.

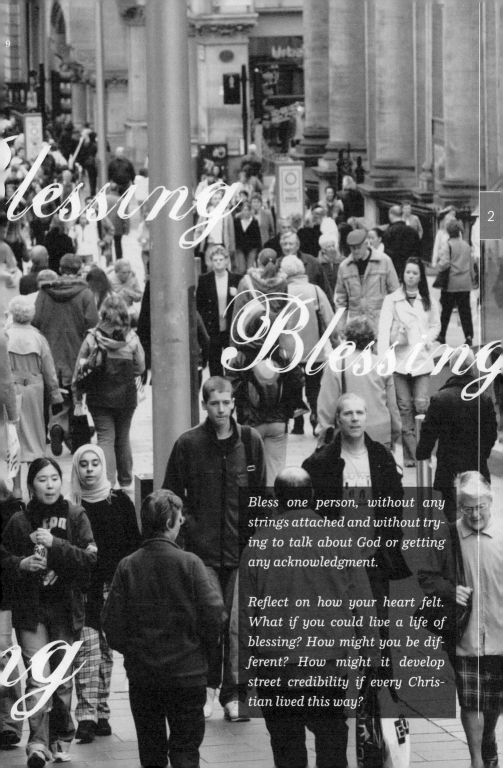

Blessing

Blessing

Bless one person, without any strings attached and without trying to talk about God or getting any acknowledgment.

Reflect on how your heart felt. What if you could live a life of blessing? How might you be different? How might it develop street credibility if every Christian lived this way?

Meet at a group member's home or some other place where you can share a meal together.

As we consider being an incarnational community, we now have to grapple with some pretty sensitive issues.

Many small groups do well studying scripture and providing a safe place for other Christians but struggle to see mission occur. The most common reason we hear goes something like this: "I'm afraid to bring a non-Christian friend to my small group."

Why is this? Well, it's simple. The group hasn't become incarnational yet. People may be consistent, good-hearted, faithful, and may even want to be missional, but it can still be hard to trust the community to have the right posture together.

Posture is the "attitude of the body." Normally this refers to physical posture, but think of it in terms of your community. In other words, what is the attitude that people pick up from your entire group?

Posture problems can show up when a guest uses language that some consider inappropriate, has a different way of parenting, or expresses an unorthodox belief system. Issues can come up related to basic life values, appropriate activities, or whose perspectives rub off on who. While there aren't always easy answers to these problems, it's easier to talk about the tension before situations occur. Your group's ability to express incarnational community depends on it.

"People may be consistent, good-hearted, faithful, and may even want to be missional, but it can still be hard to trust the community to have the right posture together."

2

Questions for group discussion:

Be as honest as you can be...

Do you feel that you could bring *anyone* to this community? Why or why not?

What are you afraid would happen if your friends were to meet each other? Hang out together? Or discuss spiritual things together?

What issues could come up that you might possibly disagree on? Make a list and begin the dialogue.

What are ways your group can navigate the balance of "whimsical holiness," that is, holding to the values of following Christ while fostering an atmosphere of non-judgment and acceptance?

NEXT WEEK...

Meet at a group member's home. Plan to share a meal and remember Christ's death and resurrection.

INCARN

What is incarnational?

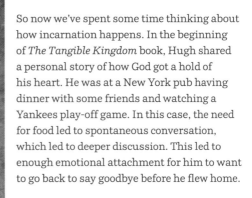

So now we've spent some time thinking about how incarnation happens. In the beginning of *The Tangible Kingdom* book, Hugh shared a personal story of how God got a hold of his heart. He was at a New York pub having dinner with some friends and watching a Yankees play-off game. In this case, the need for food led to spontaneous conversation, which led to deeper discussion. This led to enough emotional attachment for him to want to go back to say goodbye before he flew home.

The key point of the story was that while Hugh was "on his way," God set up an appointment that would forever change his future, and that of many others.

2

As we've worked through this week, you may have begun to see how to intentionalize incarnational activity. We've discovered that most God-moments are unexpected and occur along the way to someplace else. They will seem like interruptions, but if you begin to look for God's fingerprints in your day and in every relationship, in every coffee shop, in every conversation you have with your neighbor, there's a good chance you will begin to see God's incarnational presence.

TIONAL

Write down some of the people you met and events that happened along the way in your spiritual pilgrimage.

What was it about these people that drew you to them?

Identify where God is most likely to show up along the way in your daily life.

2

Think of times when you've had "bad posture" with someone. If you have the ability to communicate with any of these people, consider sending a card, an email, or even better, make an appointment to have coffee with them simply to apologize for not representing God's unconditional acceptance and love for them.

Consider: The work of the cross of Christ completely paid the price for our sins, allowing us to rest and believe what the Father says of us now, "You are forgiven!"

My God, my God, why have you forsaken me? Why are you so far from saving me, so far from the words of my groaning? O my God, I cry out by day, but you do not answer, by night, and am not silent. Yet you are enthroned as the Holy One; you are the praise of Israel. In you our fathers put their trust; they trusted and you delivered them. They cried to you and were saved; in you they trusted and were not disappointed. But I am a worm and not a man, scorned by men and despised by the people. All who see me mock me; they hurl insults, shaking their heads: "He trusts in the LORD; let the LORD rescue him. Let him deliver him, since he delights in him." Yet you brought me out of the womb; you made me trust in you even at my mother's breast. From birth I was cast upon you; from my mother's womb you have been my God. Do not be far from me, for trouble is near and there is no one to help. Many bulls surround me; strong bulls of Bashan encircle me. Roaring lions tearing their prey open their mouths wide against me. **I am poured out like water, and all my bones are out of joint. My heart has turned to wax; it has melted away within me.** My strength is dried up like a potsherd, and my tongue sticks to the roof of my mouth; you lay me in the dust of death. Dogs have surrounded me; a band of evil men has encircled me, they have pierced my hands and my feet. I can count all my bones; people

What is incarnational?

stare and gloat over me. They divide my garments among them and cast lots for my clothing. But you, O LORD, be not far off; O my Strength, come quickly to help me. Deliver my life from the sword, my precious life from the power of the dogs. Rescue me from the mouth of the lions; save me from the horns of the wild oxen. I will declare your name to my brothers; in the congregation I will praise you. You who fear the LORD, praise him! All you descendants of Jacob, honor him! Revere him, all you descendants of Israel! **For he has not despised or disdained the suffering of the afflicted one; he has not hidden his face from him but has listened to his cry for help.** From you comes the theme of my praise in the great assembly; before those who fear you will I fulfill my vows. The poor will eat and be satisfied; they who seek the LORD will praise him—may your hearts live forever! All the ends of the earth will remember and turn to the LORD, and all the families of the nations will bow down before him, for dominion belongs to the LORD and he rules over the nations. All the rich of the earth will feast and worship; all who go down to the dust will kneel before him—those who cannot keep themselves alive. Posterity will serve him; future generations will be told about the Lord. **They will proclaim his righteousness to a people yet unborn—for he has done it.** (Psalm 22)

2

These ancient words were written long before Jesus came and yet they describe in clear (and sometimes uncomfortable) terms some of the struggles inherent in living an incarnational life.

THE GOSPEL

The definition of the word *gospel* is "good news." It's a simple word for something big. In fact, the Gospel that Jesus talked about was so big that he had to give people many different teachings and practical examples. His Gospel was about a new Kingdom that would change *everything* about a person, their community, and their world.

SOMETHING'S MISSING (MATT)

A few weeks ago, I was invited to a barbecue with some people from church, some of whom I only vaguely knew. As we sat around the table enjoying the tasty burgers, I got to know the other guests a little better.

Sitting next to me at the table was a guy who had recently moved into the area. He told me about his work as a salesman and was apparently comfortable enough to announce his status as a recovering addict to a wide variety of things.

Next to him was the host for the evening. In the course of the conversation, he mentioned that he and his wife were having money problems and were worried about making the monthly mortgage payments.

His three young kids were poking in and out, clearly looking for some attention. "My oldest has been getting into fights at school," he confided. "We don't really know how to handle it."

Across the table were a guy and a girl, both single, both recent graduates from college. They swapped stories about trying to figure out their lives and the challenge of finding a good job.

A newly married couple rounded out the group. They joked about learning to squeeze the toothpaste the right way, but underneath their humor was the sense that they were having a hard time dealing with the demands of married life.

The Gospel

We've seen a recurring theme over and over again during the past few years. Even among Christians, our conversations range from politics to the economy to parenting to marriage and careers and yet, one painful reality is usually clear: the Gospel has not touched down on Planet Earth for many Christians.

When and where the Gospel lost its place in the everyday life of believers is a mystery, but there is no doubt that it is not informing most of our basic life issues, priorities and decision-making. We often end up shrinking the concept of the Gospel down to a small set of beliefs or doctrines focused primarily on the "afterlife" and they have no practical effect on our daily lives. At the same time, we neglect to live out the greater Story of God that we are all a part of.

Imagine what could change if the Good News of Jesus's life death and resurrection was allowed to shape and inform all the areas of our lives.

3.1 [EXPLORATION: NOTES]

When and how have you experienced the Good News of the Kingdom?

Is your own view of the Gospel missing anything?

The Gospel

In what ways could you expand it?

Write down how you would describe it to someone if they asked you, "So what is the Gospel?"

The Gospel

He went to Nazareth, where he had been brought up, and on the Sabbath day he went into the synagogue, as was his custom. And he stood up to read. The scroll of the prophet Isaiah was handed to him. Unrolling it, he found the place where it is written

the spirit of the sovereign lord is on me, because the lord has anointed me to preach good news to the poor.

"The Spirit of the Lord is on me, because he has anointed me to preach good news to the poor.

he has sent me to bind up the brokenhearted,

He has sent me to proclaim freedom for the prisoners and recovery of sight for the blind, to release the oppressed,

to proclaim freedom for the captives and release from darkness for the prisoners,

to proclaim the year of the Lord's favor."

to proclaim the year of the lord s favor and the day of vengeance of our god,

Then he rolled up the scroll, gave it back to the attendant and sat down. The eyes of everyone in the synagogue were fastened on him,

to comfort all who mourn, and provide for those who grieve in zion

and he began by saying to them, "Today this scripture is fulfilled in your hearing."

-- matthew 9:35-38

to bestow on them a crown of beauty instead of ashes, the oil of gladness instead of mourning, and a garment of praise instead of a spirit of despair.

Jesus went through all the towns and villages, teaching in their synagogues, preaching the good news of the kingdom and healing every disease and sickness. When he saw the crowds,

they will be called oaks of righteousness, a planting of the lord for the display of his splendor.

[isaiah 61:1-4]

he had compassion on them, because they were harassed and helpless, like sheep without a shepherd. Then he said to his disciples, "The harvest is plentiful but the workers are few. Ask the Lord of the harvest, therefore, to send out workers into his harvest field."

-- luke 4:16-22

In Isaiah, we see the need for a bigger understanding of the Gospel. In the words and actions of Jesus, we see him bringing fulfillment to God's promise of redemption and hope.

How do you think the people in the synagogue responded to Jesus' words?

What did the Good News Jesus proclaimed seem to focus on?

What does it mean for you today?

List some of the key aspects of the Gospel illustrated in the given scriptures.

3

When you think of the Gospel, what AREA(s) of your life have you most often connected it to?

What parts of your life today do you still need to apply the Gospel to?

The Gospel of the Kingdom is about movement and change. When the Good News comes into our lives and we begin to trust Jesus and his completed work on our behalf, we are brought into God's family—a community of believers—and then filled with and guided by his own Holy Spirit. Jesus said, "Peace be with you! As the Father has sent me, I am sending you." The **Gospel** creates **Community** that is sent on **Mission**.

Gospel isn't just the Good News for our afterlife; the Gospel is the beginning, middle and end of our entire journey as a Christian. If we have put our faith in Jesus, we have been saved from the penalty for our sins (justification). We are also being saved from the power of sin in our life today (sanctification). And we will be saved from the presence of sin when Jesus returns and restores all things back to the way God originally created them (glorification). The Gospel is God's power to save us but it also gives us our purpose as part of his family on mission.

Community starts in authentic ways when we are brought into a right relationship with God through the redemptive work of Jesus on the cross. We then grow in our relationship with God (worship, prayer, wisdom, knowledge, listening, seeking) and with others. The Gospel unites diverse groups of people together in Christ. The call of community isn't about finding people just like us, or excluding those who aren't. True gospel community is the result of God making us his family as we then live out our lives of love and service to each other and the world empowered by his Spirit.

Mission represents God's sending of every Christ-follower to participate in his restorative work in all aspects of life. Gospel mission reflects God's simple call to remake the world, and people's lives, back to the way he originally created them to be. Living on God's mission helps us to remember that life is not all about me and my personal happiness. It's about being and making disciples of Jesus who show the world what God is truly like. We are God's missionary family sent to serve the world through displaying and declaring this Good News.

A NEW IDENTITY: Jesus commanded that we be baptized into the name of the Father, and of the Son, and of the Holy Spirit. (Matt. 28:19). This is a baptism into a new identity. As believers, we are now sons and daughters of God and a part of his eternal family. With Jesus, the Son, now our king and Lord, we live as his servants in the world. As he served, we too should serve.

Jesus said, "As the Father has sent me, I am sending you." We now have the same Spirit living within us, sending us as missionaries into every context of life. Our identity in Christ makes us part of a family of missionary servants!

A KINGDOM LIFE LIVED ON MISSION IS REALLY ABOUT LIVING ORDINARY, EVERYDAY LIFE IN COMMUNITY, WITH GREAT GOSPEL INTENTIONALITY.

To be honest, most of us look at these three aspects of Kingdom life without much argument. We've talked about aspects of these ideas a hundred different ways, heard sermon after sermon, and have created an extensive array of programs to challenge believers to live accordingly. But truly integrating them into our lives rarely seems to happen.

The reason for this is that there are real barriers to submitting our entire lives to living in a gospel community on mission.

Galatians 5:17 says it this way: "For the sinful nature desires what is contrary to the Spirit, and the Spirit what is contrary to the sinful nature. They are in conflict with each other, so that you do not do what you want."

So if you really want to know why people just go to church without engaging the gospel in everyday life, you don't need to look far. It's not that the pace of the world is too fast or the forces of darkness are too great. It's that we're fighting against ourselves.

When you think about letting the Gospel have your whole life, what are you afraid of? What are you excited about? How might your life change if you began to look at the Gospel as the A-Z of your Christian life and not just about the beginning or the eternal future?

Consider the three aspects of Kingdom life - Gospel, Community and Mission. Place an "X" on the line to evaluate how you're doing in each area.

GOSPEL

NOT SO HOT   PRETTY GOOD

The call of the Gospel on our lives touches everything...relationships, time management, our priorities, money, sexuality...everything! It is not just about avoiding hell and getting into heaven when you die. This is what discipleship is all about—letting God bring about change in every area of our lives from the inside out.

The Gospel

COMMUNITY

NOT SO HOT   PRETTY GOOD

The call to community is more than just going to church on Sunday or a weekly "small group" meeting. A commitment to community might change the way you think about your Christian friends…and everyone else too. Instead of working to impress them with your spirituality, you might find yourself entrusting them with your struggles. Together in community with God. Which might lead to better relationships. Which might lead to you going on mission together with God. Which is the whole point.

MISSION

NOT SO HOT   PRETTY GOOD

The call to *mission* may cause you to memorize the names of everyone on your street; take new co-workers out for lunch; throw parties to connect friends who don't know each other; go out of your way to ask people, "How are things going?" You might intentionally give some money to help people or support church, civic, or global causes that meet practical needs. You might feel the call to give time to volunteer. You might even participate in local or global missions.

Looking back at the scriptures from Day 2 of this week, we are challenged by Jesus describing his own mission in very practical, concrete terms. While our ministry efforts often focus on getting people to convert to Christianity, he seems to be much more interested in helping them with what concerns them now. The Gospel does that.

His list of priorities seems surprisingly devoid of lofty spiritual concepts. Rather, by announcing himself as the fulfillment of all the promises of Isaiah 61, he steps directly into the real world of pain, disappointment, and brokenness.

This may mean big changes. It may change how we relate to the sojourners in our own lives. It may change how we think about our neighborhoods and cities. It may change our own hearts.

When we begin to understand the Gospel that Jesus was talking about, we start seeing it all around. It shows up in surprising ways and places, acted out by unexpected people. Here's a thought for you: God wants you to bring the Gospel to someone in ways that affect their life in the here and now, not just their eternal future. (Don't worry, we'll get to the eternity thing later, but stay with us!)

The Gospel

DISCOVERING THE GOSPEL IN YOUR COMMUNITY

Where is God already at work in your neighborhood? In your city?

Look for the work of the Gospel among the following people: the poor, the brokenhearted, those in captivity, the prisoners, those who are in mourning, those who are in despair. It might help to grab a telephone book or use the internet to make a list of people and organizations who are helping to bring redemption.

Watch for the Gospel in unexpected places. Is it possible that God might be using non-Christians to bring redemption to your city?

3

Make a list in the space to the left of the things you find.

DISCOVERING THE GOSPEL IN YOUR OWN LIFE

Where in your life do you interact with people from the above list?

Think about people in your neighborhood, your job, your school, and the places you spend time.

Make a list of places where your life interacts with God's activity in their lives.

BE THE GOOD NEWS

In the next few days, be "good news" to some of the people in the above lists.

Send flowers or a gift card, mow a lawn, mentor a young person, clean up a park, help someone for free—construction, decorating, babysitting, cooking. Think about blessings in these 3 categories: words, actions and gifts. Ask God to show you three people you can intentionally bless this week.

Meet at a group member's home or some other place where you can share a meal together.

Creation, Fall, Redemption, Restoration

Every person has these four parts in their story... have you ever noticed that? Remember, your story is a part of the ultimate Story—God's Story. When you are telling your story, it should end up more focused on God and how Jesus rescued and saved you. You should not end up looking like the hero in this story—God is always the hero!

Take a look at these four movements and think about how you could tell your story in light of the Gospel story. You may want to write out each "movement".

CREATION

How did your life begin? Where were you born? Tell briefly about your family, parents, how many brothers and/or sisters you have and what really began to shape who YOU were becoming as a person before you began to be a disciple of Jesus'.

The Key Question is: Who or what most shaped who you thought you were, and where you got your real value and "identity" in life from?

FALL

What was happening in your life that was "broken"—NOT the way God created it and you to be? Relationships? Health? Respect for parents, teachers, your self? What types of specific sins were you falling into and what were the effects of this? What types of things (other than trusting God) did you try to use to "fix" your life...but they didn't work?

The Key Question is: Why was your relationship with God and others, (and anything else in your life), NOT the way it was supposed to be? (like God created it...)

The Gospel

REDEMPTION

Explain how the sins you mentioned above, and the effects of these sins in your life, were rescued and redeemed by Jesus. Connect specific sins to the Gospel and how Jesus' life, death and resurrection have redeemed and restored those parts of your life back to the way God created them to be.

The Key Question is: How has Jesus paid the penalty for your sins (when He died on the Cross) and how did you come to put your faith and trust in him to save you and restore you?

3

RESTORATION

What is happening in your life now? God has redeemed you from the penalty of your sins and is now restoring you from the affects of past sins. How is God changing you, using you, speaking to you now?

The Key Question is: What has changed and is changing in your life now? And who and what is the focus of your life today? Be sure to include at least two examples of how the Gospel (Jesus at work in your life) is showing up in your everyday life and relationships as good news!

Group Discussion: Take turns telling your own Gospel stories through the lenses of Creation, Fall, Redemption, and Restoration. Tips: Keep it short. Don't get "preachy" or "churchy". Keep God and Jesus the "main characters".

NEXT WEEK...

Meet at a group member's home.
Plan to bring ingredients to make soup together.

By now, we are beginning to see clearly that God's Gospel is a lot bigger than our normal Christian experience. We've also learned that the best way to expand our Gospel story is to get together with some friends to live in gospel community on mission. There, the Kingdom will become tangible.

So what's stopping us? It's clear that the biggest hindrance is really our own hearts. Surprisingly, our struggles are often no different than the struggles that non-Christians face.

Understanding this helps us to see that until the Gospel gets bigger in our own lives, we'll have a hard time displaying and declaring it to the world. As we face this, we discover an opportunity to open ourselves to a much deeper transformation. We find ways to let God speak into every nook and cranny of our lives.

67

The biggest hindrance
to living out the Gospel

3

Make a list of things that non-Christians struggle with.

Circle the things on your list that Christians also struggle with.

Who needs the Gospel the most, the Christians or the non-Christians?

Since we all struggle with so many of the same things, how might this affect your posture toward non-Christians?

Looking back, have you been judgemental of Christians or sojourners? If so, write a prayer of confession to God. Name specifically where you want the Big Gospel to penetrate into your own life.

Consider: The work of growing "new life" in us or in others is
God's work. God may use us to scatter seeds of the Gospel, but we
can rest in his ability to bring growth.

When he was alone, the Twelve and the others around him asked him about the parables. He told them, "The secret of the kingdom of God has been given to you. But to those on the outside everything is said in parables so that, 'They may be ever seeing but never perceiving, and ever hearing but never understanding; otherwise they might turn and be forgiven!'"

Then Jesus said to them, "Don't you understand this parable? How then will you understand any parable?"

"The farmer sows the word. Some people are like seed along the path, where the word is sown. As soon as they hear it, Satan comes and takes away the word that was sown in them. Others, like seed sown on rocky places, hear the word and at once receive it with joy."

"But since they have no root, they last only a short time. When trouble or persecution comes because of the word, they quickly fall away. Still others, like seed sown among thorns, hear the word; but the worries of this life, the deceitfulness of wealth and the desires for other things come in and choke the word, making it unfruitful. Others, like seed sown on good soil, hear the word, accept it, and produce a crop—thirty, sixty or even a hundred times what was sown."

[Mark 4:10-20]

The Gospel

The seeds of the Gospel are spread everywhere.

3

WHAT IS COMMUNITY?

COMMUNITY CANNOT BE CREATED IN ISOLATION, NOR DOES IT HAPPEN WITHOUT ACTION. IT REQUIRES PEOPLE TO NAVIGATE THE TENSIONS OF INTERPERSONAL RELATIONSHIPS.

According to Webster, *community* can be defined as a unified body of individuals, a group of people with a common characteristic or interest living together within a larger society.

When we think of community, a number of words come to mind: *unified, joint, participate, love, common, cooperate, connect, sharing...*

"Community" is a word with many meanings and contexts. It's an ideal, a hope, and a need. It's the foundation of any group or church and requires people to interact, share, and participate in a common effort. It's similar to a team sport that requires individuals to prioritize the involvement of others in order to succeed.

Community cannot be created in isolation, nor does it happen without action. It requires people to navigate the tensions of interpersonal relationships.

Creating community doesn't come easily, but when it happens, the rewards are worth the effort.

What is community?

So what does community look like? Lots of people talk about it. It looks good on paper. But when it really starts to work, it sometimes shows up in unexpected ways. Here are some moments of community that we've experienced...

DISCOVERING COMMUNITY

>> People intentionally moving to other parts of the city to be closer to those in their community.

>> Communities getting together just to pray and plan their monthly calendars.

>> A sojourner inviting himself into a prayer gathering to pray and support someone who was leaving on an international missions trip.

>> Some communities focusing their benevolent action overseas, others across state lines, and others simply blessing people across the street.

>> Communities going through the good pain of sending out close friends to start another community simply because they wanted to bring mission to two or three sojourners.

>> Our older kids babysitting the younger kids at another community member's home across the street.

>> A leader of a community asking for me to come help them as they worked through some doctrinal concerns together.

>> When a member was having financial problems, the whole community taking money out of their wallets on the spot to help with her car payment.

>> Communities growing deeper through hard discussions, confrontations, and interpersonal challenges.

>> Communities offering short- and long-term housing to people in need of a place to stay.

>> Communities growing together, sometimes exchanging time at the weekly large gathering for focused time serving their neighborhood together on a Sunday morning.

4

Have you ever enjoyed a significant community experience?
Describe what it looked and felt like.

What made it so meaningful to you?

What are some positive and negative examples of community that you've experienced?

What are your biggest hopes and fears as you think about the potential of being involved in a Christian community?

Acts 2:42-47

THEY DEVOTED THEMSELVES TO THE APOSTLES' TEACHING AND TO FELLOWSHIP, TO THE BREAKING OF BREAD AND TO PRAYER.

EVERYONE WAS FILLED WITH AWE AT THE MANY WONDERS AND SIGNS PERFORMED BY THE APOSTLES. ALL THE BELIEVERS WERE TOGETHER AND HAD EVERYTHING IN COMMON. THEY SOLD PROPERTY AND POSSESSIONS TO GIVE TO ANYONE WHO HAD NEED.

EVERY DAY THEY CONTINUED TO MEET TOGETHER IN THE TEMPLE COURTS. THEY BROKE BREAD IN THEIR HOMES AND ATE TOGETHER WITH GLAD AND SINCERE HEARTS, PRAISING GOD AND ENJOYING THE FAVOR OF ALL THE PEOPLE. AND THE LORD ADDED TO THEIR NUMBER DAILY THOSE WHO WERE BEING SAVED.

I Peter 4:8-10

ABOVE ALL, LOVE EACH OTHER DEEPLY, BECAUSE LOVE COVERS OVER A MULTITUDE OF SINS. OFFER HOSPITALITY TO ONE ANOTHER WITHOUT GRUMBLING. EACH ONE SHOULD USE WHATEVER GIFT HE HAS RECEIVED TO SERVE OTHERS, FAITHFULLY ADMINISTERING GOD'S GRACE IN ITS VARIOUS FORMS.

What is community?

FOR CHRIST'S LOVE COMPELS US AND
HE DIED FOR ALL, THAT THOSE WHO
LIVE SHOULD NO LONGER LIVE FOR
THEMSELVES BUT FOR HIM WHO DIED
FOR THEM AND WAS RAISED AGAIN.
SO FROM NOW ON WE REGARD NO ONE
FROM A WORLDLY POINT OF VIEW.

2 Corinthians 5:14-16

I THANK MY GOD EVERY TIME
I REMEMBER YOU. IN ALL MY
PRAYERS FOR ALL OF YOU, I ALWAYS
PRAY WITH JOY BECAUSE OF YOUR
PARTNERSHIP IN THE GOSPEL.

Philippians 1:3

4

Community is talked about all through scripture. Whether
it's Abraham's huge family, King David's band of misfits
and mighty men, Paul's reference to the people in each
town at the end of his letters, or the passages where Jesus is
together with the disciples, the context in many scriptures
includes a deep sense of community.

Christian community is unique in that it must be based
on three primary themes: personal devotion to Jesus, the
common call or mission of the Gospel, and the inclusion of
all people, especially those who don't fit in.

*Read back through the scriptures. Circle things that stand out
to you as elements of community.*

In their day, how would people have described the God-followers like Abraham or Paul?

Describe how the disciples might have characterized the community they had with Jesus.

As you read the scriptures from the previous page, what thoughts come to mind about how you view your own community?

What would need to change to incorporate more opportunities for intentional, gospel-centered community to take place in your life?

4

In your heart?

With your time?

With your possessions?

In Acts 2 and 5 we see that the Christian community "found favor with all the people" and that they were held in high regard by all who watched their lives together. So often we think that the conversion process is dependent upon our individual witness, but the scriptures are clear...it was about THEM!

the power of they, them, and we

For the church in Thessalonica, people heard about their joy, their faith, and how they collectively turned from idols to serve the living God. Paul tells them that their common story actually "echoed" throughout the entire region. Likewise, Paul reminded the Corinthian communities that God "always leads us in triumphal procession in Christ and through us spreads everywhere the fragrance of the knowledge of him. For we are to God the aroma of Christ among those who are being saved..." (2 Corinthians 2:14-15)

Their common struggle was evident to all: They shared their food, their homes, and spontaneous life experiences together. Most importantly, they shared mission. Because of their common commitment to prioritize God's mission to the world, they were determined, consistent, hospitable, and gave priority to the community over their individual needs.

What is community?

4

here's the rub...

we all live out of individualistic values instead
of communal values.

we protect our time, prioritize our agendas.
we deal with our struggles in isolation and get
sucked into a pace of life which leaves no time
for spontaneous or intentional community.

What might you have to give up in order to make time for your community?

What are the benefits that you might gain by going deeper into community?

What personal interests, hobbies, or activities can you share with others?

How can you turn your personal devotions into communal devotions?

Write a prayer expressing your frustrations, struggles, feelings, and hopes about community.

Community is based on social interaction, but social interaction can be awkward for people. Remember how it felt to stand in a line and wait to be picked for a team? How about that weird pressure in middle school to find someone to dance with? What about your first date? How about that first office party? Have you ever entered someone's home and felt uncomfortable? Maybe the house was a mess or you picked up on a strange family vibe, like you just walked in on a fight.

So what does this tell us about community? A key component of community is hospitality. In fact, one of the definitions of hospitality is to show friendship to a visitor. The idea of "brotherly love" as described in the New Testament actually means "to love outsiders as if they were our own brothers or sisters."

Ask a few others in your community to come 15 minutes early. Have one of them answer the door. This will help people feel comfortable because it will provide them with the chance to get to know more people.

Always have some finger food, coffee, tea, or an assortment of drinks already laid out. Even if you're doing a potluck style meal or dessert, always have something laid out. Often, new people to the community are the first ones to arrive. Having something for them to eat or drink often helps relieve their tension. It also helps to hold something, like a beverage, to alleviate nervous introductions.

Try to serve your guests. Ask what each person would like to drink and serve them personally instead of expecting them to serve themselves. You can invite them to help themselves once they've gained a level of comfort in your home.

Turn the TV off (unless there's an important sporting event or something most people would be interested in).

Put music on. But not too loud.

Clean up. Vacuum.

Light candles, especially in the bathroom and in the main sitting room.

Integrate your kids into the social time but also create ways for them to grow and have fun apart from the adults.

Take time to introduce the new people to everyone.

Give people time to eat and drink together. Small talk is important to help people get to know each other.

If you're having a meal together, it can be meaningful to pray over the food and the evening before serving the food. If you're having desserts or snacks only, praying could be optional. Do what seems natural.

4

practicing hospitality
is a crucial part of building authentic community.

Meet at a group member's home where you can prepare and enjoy a meal together.

Things to do to together:

Prepare a "Community Soup" meal together using the ingredients everyone has brought.

Split up individually or in groups of two and make a list below of all the words that come to mind when you think of Community. Set a timer for five minutes.

What is community?

4

Questions for group discussion:

Read your lists. Talk about what you each think are the most important aspects of community.

Dietrich Bonhoeffer said: "*He who loves his dream of a community more than the Christian community itself becomes a destroyer of the latter, even though his personal intentions may be ever so honest and earnest and sacrificial.*" Talk about what he meant by this.

Which community ingredients are typically associated with the early church?

Which community ingredients are you most drawn to?

NEXT WEEK...

Pick a local bookstore or library for next week's meeting place. Choose one that has space to spend some time talking together.

One of the major barriers that prevents us from moving into community is *individualism*. Our culture glorifies the pioneer, the lone hero, and the overachiever, but in reality this individualism tends to work against community by prioritizing things done in isolation over things done with others.

Some of us live in places where it's common to drive an hour each way to work, where the brick walls and long driveways keep neighbors at a distance, and where spare time is commonly viewed as a rare commodity.

While we'd love to let everyone off the hook right here and say that the challenges of modern living can justify our individualism, in the grand scheme of things, it's just not the case! Our individualism is destroying the powerful, counter-cultural witness of the Church. It's limiting our capacity to experience God and it's only going to get worse unless we make some significant adjustments!

What is community?

1nd1v1dual1sm

4

List some of the things that contribute to individualism in your life.

Consider the following areas...

At work - How does your work environment contribute to individualism? Are there ways you could make changes at your job to help build community?

At home – In what ways do you tend to keep neighbors at a distance? How can you make simple adjustments to connect more with neighbors?

Time – What do you tend to do exclusively alone? How could you include others in your activities?

4

Faith – In what ways has your spiritual growth been practiced alone? How can you invite others to share in your spiritual formation?

PAUL AND TIMOTHY,

SERVANTS OF CHRIST JESUS,

TO ALL THE SAINTS IN CHRIST JESUS AT PHILIPPI, TOGETHER WITH THE OVERSEERS AND DEACONS:

GRACE AND PEACE TO YOU FROM GOD OUR FATHER AND THE LORD JESUS CHRIST. I THANK MY GOD EVERY TIME I REMEMBER YOU. IN ALL MY PRAYERS FOR ALL OF YOU, I ALWAYS PRAY WITH JOY.

BECAUSE OF YOUR PARTNERSHIP IN THE GOSPEL FROM THE FIRST DAY UNTIL NOW, BEING CONFIDENT OF THIS, THAT HE WHO BEGAN A GOOD WORK IN YOU WILL CARRY IT ON TO

COMPLETION UNTIL THE DAY OF CHRIST JESUS. IT IS RIGHT FOR ME TO FEEL THIS WAY ABOUT ALL OF YOU, SINCE I HAVE YOU IN MY HEART; FOR WHETHER I AM IN CHAINS OR DEFENDING AND CONFIRMING THE GOSPEL, ALL OF YOU SHARE IN GOD'S GRACE WITH ME. GOD CAN TESTIFY HOW I LONG FOR ALL OF YOU WITH THE AFFECTION OF CHRIST JESUS.

AND THIS IS MY PRAYER: THAT YOUR LOVE MAY ABOUND MORE AND MORE IN KNOWLEDGE AND DEPTH OF INSIGHT, SO THAT YOU MAY BE ABLE TO DISCERN WHAT IS BEST AND MAY BE PURE AND BLAMELESS UNTIL THE DAY OF CHRIST, FILLED WITH THE FRUIT OF RIGHTEOUSNESS THAT COMES THROUGH JESUS CHRIST, TO THE GLORY AND PRAISE OF GOD. [PHILIPPIANS 1:1-11]

4

Paul's greeting in Philippians 1 is a beautiful expression of community. His love for the people in Philippi is clear and so is his full commitment to their growth and good. He was anything but a disconnected individualist or distant leader. Rather, he was fully engaged in moving with them toward the completion of God's good work and was hopeful of sharing with them in God's eternal grace.

LIVING OUT

Welcome to Week 5 of the primer! By now you may be discovering some new things about the Gospel and about what it means to be a follower of Christ. It may be stirring up a lot of thoughts and feelings for you. You may also be wondering how to apply it all to your own life.

Living out is where all of this meets the real world. Living out is the natural and deliberate process of living among, listening to, and loving people in culture with the desire to connect them to our Christian community. As we learn to live the missional and incarnational way, we soon are faced with challenges to our daily living.

As we learn to live out the Gospel, we grapple with the bottom-line issue of our willingness to take responsibility for our relationships with others and whether we'll let the mission of God dictate the purpose and schedule of our lives. Inside the tension of living out are our own ambitions, our faith, our fear, and our frailty.

"Is This My Church?" (Hugh)

After about 12 months in Denver, we had been having a group of young Starbucks employees over on Saturdays to talk about life and God. Many of their conversion stories were well on the way, but we were caught off guard by a question of a young woman one night. As twenty of us were jammed in my living room, she held up her hand and asked, "Is this my church?"

I looked at my wife Cheryl across the room and clearly saw her eyes communicate, "You'd better not say yes!"

Then I looked at Matt, my ministry partner, and saw the same look.

Thinking quickly, I said, "Um, no, this is not your church, this is your...hmm...faith community...yeah...your faith community." (A beautiful, non-committal response!) "Well," she said, "I have come to faith, so aren't I supposed to have a church?"

Again, thinking on my feet, "Well, a church would be different. A church would be if we all decide to go on mission for God together. So far, we have been on mission for you. We open up our home. We buy food. We throw cool parties. We give our time to mentor you. If you all decide to be a church, you'll have to do that for everyone else. You'll have to die to your own lives like we have."

"That'll scare them out of doing church," I thought to myself. But the next week, they all decided they wanted to die with us. "Great!" I thought. Well, not really.

The following evening, Cheryl and I, and Matt and Maren sat together on our porch and lamented what giving our energy and time to this new church would cost. We were broke. Our schedules were full already. We didn't want to experience the pain of carrying the burden of leading people again. We didn't want to have to "go to church" anymore. I didn't want the pressure of preaching or preparing sermons, counseling, or losing time with my family.

5

Considering the relationships that God has brought into your life, what are your responsibilities to them now?

What would happen if you decided to give up your responsibility?

How has your faith developed as you've allowed the mission of God to shape your relationships with others?

Consider the people in your life that would benefit from your involvement. Describe how you might be able to help in their spiritual development.

Now Moses was tending the flock of Jethro, his father-in-law, the priest of Midian, and he led the flock to the far side of the desert and came to Horeb, the mountain of God. There the angel of the LORD appeared to him in flames of fire from within a bush. Moses saw that though the bush was on fire it did not burn up. So Moses thought, "I will go over and see this strange sight—why the bush does not burn up."

When the LORD saw that he had gone over to look, God called to him from within the bush, "Moses! Moses!" And Moses said, "Here I am." "Do not come any closer," God said. "Take off your sandals, for the place where you are standing is holy ground." Then he said, "I am the God of your father, the God of Abraham, the God of Isaac and the God of Jacob." At this, Moses hid his face, because he was afraid to look at God.

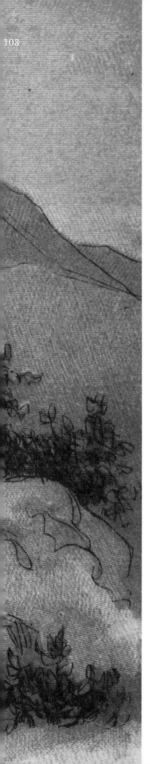

The LORD said, "I have indeed seen the misery of my people in Egypt. I have heard them crying out because of their slave drivers, and I am concerned about their suffering...I am sending you to Pharaoh to bring my people the Israelites out of Egypt." But Moses said to God, "Who am I, that I should go to Pharaoh and bring the Israelites out of Egypt?" And God said, "I will be with you. And this will be the sign to you that it is I who have sent you: When you have brought the people out of Egypt, you will worship God on this mountain."

Moses said to God, "Suppose I go to the Israelites and say to them, 'The God of your fathers has sent me to you,' and they ask me, 'What is his name?' Then what shall I tell them?" God said to Moses, "I am who I am. This is what you are to say to the Israelites: 'I AM has sent me to you.'"

Moses answered, "What if they do not believe me or listen to me and say, 'The LORD did not appear to you'?" Then the LORD said to him, "What is that in your hand?" "A staff," he replied. The LORD said, "Throw it on the ground." Moses threw it on the ground and it became a snake, and he ran from it. Then the LORD said to him, "Reach out your hand and take it by the tail." So Moses reached out and took hold of the snake and it turned back into a staff in his hand. "This," said the LORD, "is so that they may believe that the LORD, the God of their fathers—the God of Abraham, the God of Isaac and the God of Jacob—has appeared to you."

Moses said to the LORD, "O Lord, I have never been eloquent, neither in the past nor since you have spoken to your servant. I am slow of speech and tongue." The LORD said to him, "Who gave man his mouth? Who makes him deaf or mute? Who gives him sight or makes him blind? Is it not I, the LORD? Now go; I will help you speak and will teach you what to say."

But Moses said, "O Lord, please send someone else to do it."

- selections from Exodus 3 & 4

5

How do you relate with Moses when you think about living out your own calling?

Have you ever felt unqualified to live it out?

What are some excuses that you've used with God?

Describe a time when you've said to God, "Please send someone else."

5

Moses was being sent back to his own people. Assuming God is likely to send you to people who you already know, who would you be sent to?

The story of Moses reveals that it's quite natural to skirt God's calling for our lives. Despite our desire to be used by God, we often get paralyzed by insecurity.

Sometimes it's due to a lack of experience. Other times it's based on our own failures or personal issues of brokeness.

God is not caught off guard by any of these.

As you read the verses from 2 Corinthians, notice that the mark of true ministry is not perfection or results. In fact, Paul calls us "jars of clay," indicating that he knew that imperfect people would be the ones carrying the responsibility of sharing, showing, and inviting people into Kingdom life.

FOR WE DO NOT PREACH OURSELVES, BUT JESUS CHRIST AS LORD, AND OURSELVES AS YOUR SERVANTS FOR JESUS' SAKE. FOR GOD, WHO SAID, "LET LIGHT SHINE OUT OF DARKNESS," MADE HIS LIGHT SHINE IN OUR HEARTS TO GIVE US THE LIGHT OF THE KNOWLEDGE OF THE GLORY OF GOD IN THE FACE OF CHRIST.

BUT WE HAVE THIS TREASURE IN JARS OF CLAY TO SHOW THAT THIS ALL-SURPASSING POWER IS FROM GOD AND NOT FROM US.

WE ARE HARD PRESSED ON EVERY SIDE, BUT NOT CRUSHED; PERPLEXED, BUT NOT IN DESPAIR; PERSECUTED, BUT NOT ABANDONED; STRUCK DOWN, BUT NOT DESTROYED. WE ALWAYS CARRY AROUND IN OUR BODY THE DEATH OF JESUS, SO THAT THE LIFE OF JESUS MAY ALSO BE REVEALED IN OUR BODY. FOR WE WHO ARE ALIVE ARE ALWAYS BEING GIVEN OVER TO DEATH FOR JESUS' SAKE, SO THAT HIS LIFE MAY BE REVEALED IN OUR MORTAL BODY. SO THEN, DEATH IS AT WORK IN US, BUT LIFE IS AT WORK IN YOU. [2 CORINTHIANS 4:1-12]

5

When you read this, do you tend to focus on the possibilities of ministry or your clay pot?

What are your weaknesses?

How does faith enable us to take on responsibility for God's mission?

What type of burning bush is God using to get your attention right now?

5

It's normal to feel some tension related to "living out." Living on mission can be challenging. It isn't always immediately clear what we're supposed to do.

For some of that tension, it's important to remind ourselves that keeping track of the results is not our job. In fact, our main concern is to live in such a way that the Good News is clearly expressed through our lives. We trust the work of God to do the rest.

Listed to the right are six **rhythms of life** that are happening in every context and culture. In many ways you are already living in these rhythms and may not have noticed. Now we want to grow in the ability to express our gospel identity (a family of missionary servants) through every area of our lives. Take a look and think about what they might mean for you as a part of your daily and weekly rhythm of life.

Know the story

Get more and more familiar with the Bible as one big story—God's story. Get to know the stories of the people in your community and help each other see how your stories intersect and mirror God's story.

Listen

Set aside regular times to just listen to God. Listen 'backward' through time in God's Word. You can actively listen 'forward' to hear what God is saying to you today through his Spirit and through your community.

Celebrate

Gather throughout the week with your community to share stories and celebrate all that God is doing in and amongst you. Invite others to these celebrations as a way of displaying God's extravagant blessings.

Bless

Intentionally bless others through words, gifts or actions. God desires that all nations—all people—would be blessed through Jesus. Seek God's direction for who he would have you tangibly bless each week.

Eat

Regularly eat meals with others as a reminder of our common need for God and his faithfulness to provide both physically and spiritually. Try and eat one meal each week with at least one sojourner enjoying the meal with you.

ReCreate

Take time each week to rest, play, create and restore beauty in ways that display the Gospel, resting in Jesus' completed work on our behalf. Cultivate this Gospel rhythm of rest and create—ReCreate—in your life.

Get out of your house with the purpose of connecting with someone. Be creative. Here are some ideas:

- Spend some time with a friend who is having a rough week.
- Take your kids to a park or playground where there are other families to build friendships with.
- Help a neighbor with a project or chore.
- Using a hobby or personal interest, find a way to make new relationships with sojourners.
- Invite others to join a personal or family meal.
- Respond willingly to at least one interruption that comes along this week.

5

*Meet at a local bookstore or library. Choose a location that has
space for you to spend some time talking together.*

Things to do together:

Look at the Rhythms listed on the last two pages. Sit together and discuss
each of these. Try and come up with at least two or three ways you could
begin to live your life through these Rhythms as a community together.

Make a list of the ones you agree on.

5

Questions for group discussion:

Describe regular activities within each of these Rhythms that you are already doing as a community. Which of these activities could be done with greater gospel intentionality?

NEXT WEEK...

Meet at a group member's home.
Make fondue. Yes, we mean it.

The great theologian Sheryl Crow sings this line: "It's not having what you want, it's wanting what you've got." When it comes to consumerism, she's got it just about right. Consumerism is the belief that happiness comes from getting what we want or think we need. Instead of caring about the needs of others, this perspective causes us to focus primarily on our own happiness.

In fact, one of the main barriers to communion with Christ is our consumerism. Consumerism turns our focus back on ourselves and our own desires and reverses the flow toward mission. But ideally, as we enter into true communion with Christ, we are naturally drawn into mission.

Transformation in our own lives compels us to reach out to others. Following Christ into mission is a natural outgrowth of the Gospel, but it requires intentionally working against our own desires and selfish ambitions. To put it plainly, living out will require that you get over yourself and start considering the needs of others.

consumerism

Think about the condition of your communion with Christ.
Describe some of the areas in your life where consumerism might
be getting in the way.

List some ways you can deepen your communion with Christ. How
might these changes lead you further into mission?

Write down some practical changes you could make to help reduce the attitude of consumerism in your life. Here are some questions to help you get creative...

What can you do to bless others instead of waiting for others to bless you? Where can you serve where others are presently serving you? What free time can you give to reach out to others?

5

Consider: God asks us to give our entire lives to him. He wants it all. He modeled this for us when he sent his own Son to rescue us. Jesus gave everything that he might now live his life in and through us. We are his most valuable possession and he is ours!

JESUS, GRILLED BY THE PHARISEES ON WHEN THE KINGDOM OF GOD WOULD COME, ANSWERED, "THE KINGDOM OF GOD DOESN'T COME BY COUNTING THE DAYS ON THE CALENDAR. NOR WHEN SOMEONE SAYS, 'LOOK HERE!' OR, 'THERE IT IS!' AND WHY? BECAUSE GOD'S KINGDOM IS ALREADY AMONG YOU."

HE WENT ON TO SAY TO HIS DISCIPLES, "THE DAYS ARE COMING WHEN YOU ARE GOING TO BE DESPERATELY HOMESICK FOR JUST A GLIMPSE OF ONE OF THE DAYS OF THE SON OF MAN, AND YOU WON'T SEE A THING. AND THEY'LL SAY TO YOU, 'LOOK OVER THERE!' OR, 'LOOK HERE!' DON'T FALL FOR ANY OF THAT NONSENSE. THE ARRIVAL OF THE SON OF MAN IS NOT SOMETHING YOU GO OUT TO SEE. HE SIMPLY COMES.

"YOU KNOW HOW THE WHOLE SKY LIGHTS UP FROM A SINGLE FLASH OF LIGHTNING? THAT'S HOW IT WILL BE ON THE DAY OF THE SON OF MAN. BUT FIRST IT'S NECESSARY THAT HE SUFFER MANY THINGS AND BE TURNED DOWN BY THE PEOPLE OF TODAY.

"THE TIME OF THE SON OF MAN WILL BE JUST LIKE THE TIME OF NOAH -- EVERYONE CARRYING ON AS USUAL, HAVING A GOOD TIME RIGHT UP TO THE DAY NOAH BOARDED THE SHIP. THEY SUSPECTED NOTHING UNTIL THE FLOOD HIT AND SWEPT EVERYTHING AWAY.

"IT WAS THE SAME IN THE TIME OF LOT--THE PEOPLE CARRYING ON, HAVING A GOOD TIME, BUSINESS AS USUAL RIGHT UP TO THE DAY LOT WALKED OUT OF SODOM AND A FIRESTORM SWEPT DOWN AND BURNED EVERYTHING TO A CRISP. THAT'S HOW IT WILL BE--SUDDEN, TOTAL--WHEN THE SON OF MAN IS REVEALED.

"WHEN THE DAY ARRIVES AND YOU'RE OUT WORKING IN THE YARD, DON'T RUN INTO THE HOUSE TO GET ANYTHING. AND IF YOU'RE OUT IN THE FIELD, DON'T GO BACK AND GET YOUR COAT. REMEMBER WHAT HAPPENED TO LOT'S WIFE! IF YOU GRASP AND CLING TO LIFE ON YOUR TERMS, YOU'LL LOSE IT, BUT IF YOU LET THAT LIFE GO, YOU'LL GET LIFE ON GOD'S TERMS. [LUKE 17:20-33, THE MESSAGE]

5

INVITING IN

FRIENDS, NOT "TARGETS" (MATT)

Not long after moving to Denver, our missional community threw a surprise birthday party for Hugh's wife, Cheryl. We invited a number of Cheryl's friends to a nice dinner at a local restaurant. Some were from the kids' hockey association, others were friends from the neighborhood.

At the party, my wife and I were seated next to a couple of the neighbors. Since many of the families knew that Hugh and I worked together, one of their first questions was, "What does Hugh do?"

It was not a surprising question. Anyone would probably assume Hugh was a Russian spy if they didn't know his life. He just seems to

always be around, mowing the lawn or working around the house at "strange" hours of the day. He pops out at the most opportune times to lend a hand or engage in a conversation.

What was clear was that they were not there just because Hugh, the Russian spy/evangelistic missionary, had "witnessed" to them or hit them over the head with his Jesus stick.

In fact, most of them had no idea what he did for work. The reason they were at the party that night was because they knew Cheryl and Hugh to be people who were compassionate and hospitable, involved with their kids and in the community, willing to engage in real conversations about life.

123

We bring this story up for two reasons. First, it's worth noting that the majority of the people at this party were friends with Cheryl— the wife of Hugh, mother of three, hockey enthusiast, homemaker, part-time barista and real estate agent. This is significant because most people mistakenly assume that it takes a full-time minister to create a missional community. In fact, we've found that hospitality and friendship are often the quickest paths to creating environments where saint and sojourner can experience God together.

Second, we bring this up because the birthday party was the result of a natural process of connecting with folks in our circle of relationships. Most of these people would never have walked into a church building on their own. They were drawn to our missional community through our willingness to let our lives overlap with theirs. But over time these relationships laid the foundations for a very real community of faith.

INVITING IN IS INTEGRATING SOJOURNERS INTO THE COMMUNITY AS A RESULT OF LIVING OUT THE GOSPEL WITH INTENTIONAL HOSPITALITY AND COMPASSION.

6

Creating opportunities for people to participate in the Christian community is a key part of building the tangible kingdom of God. When we see people outside, we go outside to talk. When a block party invitation is given, we go, or we host one. When the snows fall hard, we shovel everyone's sidewalk. When a neighbor's child is in a school play or athletic event, we show up to support them. We're the ones that bake holiday cookies for co-workers and neighbors.

As we learned last week, we do this in the regular rhythm of life as our calling and without any strings attached. When you do this, eventually you'll find that people start to move toward you and the "inviting in" process begins.

For many of us, the challenge to "witness" and "win converts" in many of our church experiences involved doing something that was uncomfortable and seemed unnatural. As you can tell from this story, there's another way.

Hearing Hugh and Cheryl's story, what do you think they did to develop the relationships to this point?

How are you making yourself available to the people around you?

125

Who are some of the people in your life that you are currently investing in relationally?

Have you invited any of them to share a meal with you recently?

6

Jesus entered Jericho and was passing through. A man was there by the name of Zacchaeus; he was a chief tax collector and was wealthy.

He wanted to see who Jesus was, but being a short man he could not, because of the crowd. So he ran ahead and climbed a sycamore-fig tree to see him, since Jesus was coming that way.

When Jesus reached the spot, he looked up and said to him, "Zacchaeus, come down immediately. I must stay at your house today." So he came down at once and welcomed him gladly.

All the people saw this and began to mutter, "He has gone to be the guest of a 'sinner.'"

But Zacchaeus stood up and said to the Lord, "Look, Lord! Here and now I give half of my possessions to the poor, and if I have cheated anybody out of anything, I will pay back four times the amount."

Jesus said to him, "Today salvation has come to this house, because this man, too, is a son of Abraham. For the Son of Man came to seek and to save what was lost."

[Luke 19:1-10]

This week, let this thought motivate you: people are watching you! Individually and as a community you are a picture of what God is like to people...a display of the Gospel. How's that picture looking?

It's a privilege and responsibility to understand that whether it's your children, your spouse, neighbors, co-workers, Starbucks baristas, or friends you've been hanging with for years, your life is a book about God.

6

You can fake some things, but time always reveals who you are and how important God is in your life. If people find a chapter in the story of your life they can identify with or find help from, they will move toward you...and toward God.

The opposite is also true. If the story you tell through your life is not compelling, if it's not authentic, or if they can't see themselves in it, they'll find a different tree to climb.

You are always in "discipleship mode". As people watch your life and actions you are either discipling them toward a life of trusting in God or toward a life of trusting in self.

Over the last few years, who are the people that have been close enough to watch your life? (In your home, neighborhood, work, community...)

A thought--Our marriages, families and relationships have all been given to us by God primarily to show the world what he is truly like. How accurate and consistent has the Good News of the Kingdom-- the Gospel--been displayed in your life?

Have you done anything that you're now ashamed of or wish you could have changed?

What do you hope people see in your life? What opportunities are there for this to happen?

6

UNBELIEVER IS INVITED TO CHURCH

UNBELIEVER CONFESSES BELIEF

UNBELIEVER REPEATS A PRAYER

BELIEVER JOINS CHURCH

COGNITIVE DISCIPLESHIP

FOCUS: COUNTING CONFESSIONS

BELIEVING ENABLES BELONGING

Attractional

SOJOURNER IS INVITED TO BELONG

SOJOURNER CONFESSES INTEREST

SOJOURNER EXPERIENCES

THE GOOD NEWS

SOJOURNER PARTICIPATES

IN COMMUNITY

EXPERIENTIAL APPRENTICESHIP

FOCUS: TRANSFORMATION

BELONGING ENABLES BELIEVING

Incarnational

If people have been watching you and have discovered something they like, they'll eventually be watching your community. One person is a good witness, but a whole community is much more powerful.

Most churches think of their mission as creating a *place* that is attractive to unbelievers. This usually doesn't provide people with much time for observation and relationship. It is more focused on moving people across the line into belief. Once they're in, they are then "rewarded" with relationship.

6

In contrast, notice how the incarnational approach tries first to create a relational environment to which sojourners can belong so that they can feel or see aspects of the Gospel lived out. This kind of approach gives a curious sojourner ample "Zacchaeus tree time," or time to learn about and be transformed by this community called the Kingdom of God.

[read more about the attractional/incarnational contrast in *The Tangible Kingdom*, chapter 10]

What was the process by which you came to faith?

Think about the definition of a sojourner – "a spiritually curious God-seeker or a traveler who has intersected the missional community." As you consider your relationship with sojourners, where are they at in the process?

In two weeks, we'll be challenging your community to throw a party for friends and sojourners. This is step 1 of the incarnational approach – "sojourners invited to belong." As you start to think about inviting non-Christians to your party, do you feel any pressure or tension?

How might this change the way you plan for the evening?

How might you pray?

What are some practical ways you can help to create an atmosphere of belonging?

6

Imagine Zaccheus as Jesus tells him that he is coming over. Zaccheus is excited about his guest, but he's probably scared to death to have his life exposed. His house was going to reflect all the money he had made at the expense of other people. Basically, he was fearful to expose his life because it exposed his sin. No wonder he so quickly offered to sell half of his possessions. Zach was cleaning house!

If you are serious about letting the Gospel transform your life, one of the things that will happen is that it will begin to expose some areas of sin. Have you begun to experience this? If so, what is being exposed? What do you need to repent of?

Here are some areas to think about: relationships with family and friends, personal integrity, use of time, money, sex, anger, selfishness, sinful motives, pride, judgemental attitudes, hypocritical thinking.

Have a big housecleaning day. Get rid of the junk. Give the useful things away, have a yard sale, or sell them on craigslist. Save the money and use it to bless someone.

Meet at a group member's home. We suggest making fondue (a good community exercise!) Try not to catch anything on fire.

Things to do together:

Read through the scriptures listed below. Talk about the things that God values and what these values might look like in the context of your own community.

Genesis 12:1-3   *2 Timothy 2:2*
Matthew 25:34-40   *Titus 2:7-8*
Acts 2:42-45   *1 Peter 2:11-12*
Acts 13:1-3   *1 Peter 4:9*
Acts 16:13-15   *1 Peter 4:10*
Romans 12:1-2   *1 John 3:16-18*
Philippians 2:1-2   *Matthew 28:18-20*

The Intuitive Life

6

NEXT WEEK...

*Go out for a meal or coffee together next week. Pick someplace
where you can do some Bible study together.*

Prior to meeting Jesus, Zacchaeus likely had very few friends. He was a tax collector after all! When Jesus called him down from the tree, Zacchaeus was being introduced to the entire community of Jesus' followers. So Jesus, in a single moment of invitation and challenge, was drawing Zacchaeus into community and simultaneously calling him into mission.

In past weeks, we've seen how consumerism inhibits our communion with Christ and how individualism can prevent us from participating in community. Here in the story of Zacchaeus, we see Jesus pointing out one of the primary barriers that anyone can face when he or she begins to move into mission. This barrier is *materialism*.

materialism

In our own lives, materialism plays the same role as it did with Zacchaeus. When we are caught up in materialism, our communities suffer. When we are buried in debt or concerned about our "stuff," we lack time to build significant, deep relationships with each other. Our lives will begin to focus on things like security and competing with our neighbors for status and control rather than on the good news of the Gospel. To put it plainly, materialism poisons community.

whose 'stuff' is your stuff anyway? where did it all come from? who ultimately gave it to you?

Materialism is the belief that the quality of one's life is defined by what someone owns. This belief is what drives people to work too hard and neglect the important things. It will limit a person's ability to experience community or extend the Kingdom in very clear ways.

6

Just like Zacchaeus, our response to God and his community should be a deliberate move to remove our own barriers to mission.

Make a list of things you could get rid of in order to free yourself from materialism.

Describe some adjustments you can make in the following areas --

How much you work

What you spend your money on

How much you give away

A certain ruler asked him, "Good teacher, what must I do to inherit eternal life?"

"Why do you call me good?" Jesus answered. "No one is good—except God alone. You know the commandments: 'Do not commit adultery, do not murder, do not steal, do not give false testimony, honor your father and mother.'"

"All these I have kept since I was a boy," he said.

When Jesus heard this, he said to him, "You still lack one thing. Sell everything you have and give to the poor, and you will have treasure in heaven. Then come, follow me."

When he heard this, he became very sad, because he was a man of great wealth.

Jesus looked at him and said, "How hard it is for the rich to enter the kingdom of God! Indeed, it is easier for a camel to go through the eye of a needle than for a rich man to enter the kingdom of God."

Those who heard this asked, **"WHO THEN CAN BE SAVED?"**

6

Jesus replied, **"WHAT IS IMPOSSIBLE WITH MEN IS POSSIBLE WITH GOD"**
[Luke 18:18-27]

BECOMING AN
APPRENTICE

Becoming an apprentice

When you think about what it means to be a disciple of Christ, what comes to mind? Typically, when we ask this question in church groups we often get the generic responses like studying the Bible, prayer, attending church, or being involved in a small group.

In contrast, if you would have asked some of the first disciples what it was like being one of Jesus' students, they probably would have responded with, "He always tested our faith and our motives. He always took us to places we wouldn't have gone ourselves. We became friends with people we would have hated before. Looking back, it was the most wildly transforming process I could have ever imagined. I'll never be the same."

Discipleship for the disciples was different from our idea in one major way: it actually involved following Jesus where he went and doing what he did.

This brings us face-to-face with the question of how to replicate the process of discipleship. Throughout history, it has been approached in a number of ways. Some engaged in a monastic life. Others became crusaders. Some took vows of celibacy. There were many who devoted themselves to cross-cultural missions. Still others chose to live among the poor, the diseased and the outcasts of society.

In our modern era, we have in many instances reduced the discipleship process to a passive act of being taught about Jesus or studying others in history that have modeled true discipleship.

This gap between learning and action has handicapped the modern church by producing passive "disciples". We have taken discipleship off the streets and brought it into the classroom and the church pew.

While it is good to *learn about* becoming a disciple, there is significantly more that can only be understood through *practice*. In order to re-engage the discipleship process, we need to look at another word that better captures the essence of discipleship today. That word is *apprenticeship*.

LEARNING THE CRAFT (MATT)

Apprenticeship has been a significant part of my life's journey, and has been a practice that I desire to understand due to its implications on how we lead, model, train, develop, and disciple others in the ways of Christ.

I first learned about apprenticeship as a college student working as an industrial electrician. I was enrolled in a university studying electrical engineering, learning all the theory and fundamentals of how electricity worked. But it wasn't until I started using my hands and tools to create pathways for the electricity to travel that I truly began to understand the way electricity worked and flowed.

Several years later, I began working for a cabinet builder and experienced my second pure apprenticeship process. When I first started building cabinets, I was relegated to the extremely dusty duty of finish sanding. As I made three passes over every piece of wood, I learned the feel for different woods and how to take out all the imperfections without creating my own swirl marks in the process.

After gaining a feel for the wood, I began making my rounds on each piece of machinery in the shop: the table saw, the planer, the edge sander, the router, the joiner, and the radial arm saw. I learned how to measure the wood and make cuts to within 1/64th of an inch. I learned to appreciate the beauty of the wood and in the process was being apprenticed in the craft of woodworking.

7

APPRENTICESHIP IS BEST UNDERSTOOD IN THE CONTEXT OF LEARNING A TRADE, ESPECIALLY ONE THAT **REQUIRES DEVELOPING A SET OF SKILLS** IMPORTANT TO BECOMING A FINE CRAFTSMAN.

Describe an apprenticeship environment that you have experienced.

Have you ever had someone apprentice you in your faith? If so, describe the process and what you learned.

Describe some differences between classroom learning and apprenticeship? It might help to make a chart with two columns - class and apprenticeship.

7

DO NOT MERELY LISTEN TO THE WORD, AND SO
DECEIVE YOURSELVES. DO WHAT IT SAYS. ANYONE
WHO LISTENS TO THE WORD BUT DOES NOT DO
WHAT IT SAYS IS LIKE A MAN WHO LOOKS AT
HIS FACE IN A MIRROR AND, AFTER LOOKING AT
HIMSELF, GOES AWAY AND IMMEDIATELY FORGETS
WHAT HE LOOKS LIKE. BUT THE MAN WHO LOOKS
INTENTLY INTO THE PERFECT LAW THAT GIVES
FREEDOM, AND CONTINUES TO DO THIS, NOT
FORGETTING WHAT HE HAS HEARD, BUT DOING IT
HE WILL BE BLESSED IN WHAT HE DOES.

[JAMES 1:22-25]

Becoming an apprentice

THEN JESUS SAID TO HIS DISCIPLES, "IF ANYONE WOULD COME AFTER ME, HE MUST DENY HIMSELF AND TAKE UP HIS CROSS AND FOLLOW ME. FOR WHOEVER WANTS TO SAVE HIS LIFE WILL LOSE IT, BUT WHOEVER LOSES HIS LIFE FOR ME WILL FIND IT. WHAT GOOD WILL IT BE FOR A MAN IF HE GAINS THE WHOLE WORLD, YET FORFEITS HIS SOUL? OR WHAT CAN A MAN GIVE IN EXCHANGE FOR HIS SOUL? FOR THE SON OF MAN IS GOING TO COME IN HIS FATHER'S GLORY WITH HIS ANGELS, AND THEN HE WILL REWARD EACH PERSON ACCORDING TO WHAT HE HAS DONE.

[MATTHEW 16:24-27]

I TELL YOU THE TRUTH, ANYONE WHO HAS FAITH IN ME WILL DO WHAT I HAVE BEEN DOING. HE WILL DO EVEN GREATER THINGS THAN THESE, BECAUSE I AM GOING TO THE FATHER.

[JOHN 14:12]

Throughout the gospels there are numerous accounts of apprenticeship in action. We often refer to this process as *discipleship* because the disciples were among those being trained. The problem is that what we call discipleship today is nothing like what they went through. The disciples of Jesus were being trained by living example. And they were being trained in action, not just in theory.

It's surprising, then, that much of what we call discipleship training involves learning concepts individually with little emphasis on the practical implementation of the knowledge. Not only has discipleship become passive, but it has also been tailored to fit the consumer lifestyle. It costs very little in most contexts to become a disciple—attending a class, completing a workbook, or completing a program. What we need is a new definition of discipleship. What if discipleship became more costly in terms of time, effort, relationships, or finances? What if *discipleship* became a real *apprenticeship* in community?

7

In most apprenticeship environments, the apprentice gets paid very little and is required to work very hard in order to master the trade. A good example is the process of becoming a physician. Years of schooling and practice are required before one can be called a doctor. In a similar way, when Jesus said, "Follow me and I will make you fishers of men," there was an understanding of the personal cost. For most, it meant leaving family, jobs, stable income, and a willingness to give up years of their lives to follow Jesus.

As you consider the differences between passive discipleship and active apprenticeship, how would you describe your own Christian journey so far?

In all actuality, you cannot really become a mature disciple or "master apprentice" of Jesus without Gospel, Community and Mission. We need all three.

Apart from the Gospel, our communities can end up self-focused or based on any number of things besides the Kingdom. A social club of sorts. One-to-one discipleship can produce aspects of Christ-likeness in us, but without a community that is made up of all the different parts of the Body of Christ "rubbing up against" our areas of sin and unbelief we will never grow into a fuller picture of Jesus.

And it is when we live life in community out on mission, displaying and declaring the Gospel and making more apprentices of Jesus that we truly grow. Sitting in a classroom or living room week after week will never produce the kind of radical transformation the Kingdom calls us to.

Becoming an apprentice

In what ways is this different than how you thought about your spiritual growth or the ways you were "discipled" in the past?

Are you willing to engage, or re-engage, your spiritual life as an apprentice in a gospel-centered community on mission? What would need to change in order to fully pursue being an apprentice of Jesus in this way?

7

Discipleship is the holistic care of a smaller group of people who are consistently experiencing Jesus' life and teaching together in a healthy environment where they are learning to submit every area of life to the Lordship of Jesus.

What kind of environment did Jesus create to develop his disciples?

Take a look at these passages from the Bible and observe how Jesus made disciples. Ask these questions as you read:

What were they doing? Where? How often? With whom? How is this part of Jesus making disciples?

Matthew 4:19
Matthew 5:1-12
Matthew 9:9-13, 35-38
Matthew 10:5-8
Matthew 20:20-28
Matthew 28:19-20
Luke 6:39-42
Luke 8:1
Luke 9:28
Luke 10:1-3
Luke 14:1-6
Luke 17:11-14
John 14:26
John 16:7-15

This is a good time to talk to God about your hopes (and his hopes) for your growth. Thank him for his grace with your failures, but even more, thank him for the hope he gives you for the future.

Write a prayer expressing your thoughts and feelings to God.

7

Many of us have experienced a faith focused on "sin management." That is, we focus on *not doing* things God has asked us to avoid. But have you ever considered that sin can also include "not doing" the good things God has asked us to do? We may feel bad if we use a swear word but not care at all if we forget to encourage a friend.

If apprenticeship is about becoming like Jesus, we'll have to start looking at a much broader context for faithful living.

To be honest, we're not really into checklists. Still, they can sometimes be useful in looking at God's larger hopes for us—and in gracefully critiquing where we need to grow. On the next page we listed some questions that will help expand your understanding of what God is trying to produce in and through you. As you read through them, make some notes about how you are doing as an apprentice. It may be helpful to circle the areas where you hope to see growth.

Are your prayers monologues or dialogues?

Are you able to describe the story of your faith
  in Christ to others?

Do you feel comfortable participating
  in activities with non-Christians?

Are you consistently involved in a Christian community?

Are you committed to spending time regularly
  with others in your community?

Do you regularly welcome others into your home?

Do you have a hobby that you practice regularly with others?

Do you give your money to bless others?

Are you able to control your temper and your words?

Is sharing your life with others a priority for you?

Are there people in your community who are aware of your vices?

Do you have a wise mentor who guides you through tough decisions?

Are you in the habit of scripture reading and reflection?

Do you prayerfully allow God to guide your week?

Do you consider spending time with your family as part of God's mission?

7

This is a good time to talk to God about your hopes (and his hopes) for your growth. Thank him for his grace with your failures, but even more, thank him for the hope he gives you for the future.

Spend some time in prayer expressing your thoughts and feelings to God.

Go out for a meal or coffee together. If there are kids, make sure they have something fun to do. Bring a Bible.

If we are to take apprenticeship with Christ seriously, we need the input and guidance of our entire community along with people who are "masters" in various areas of faith, living out the gospel in community together on mission.

Things to do together: Reflecting on the scriptures you read yesterday, discuss these different aspects of a healthy discipleship or "apprenticeship" environment.

Empowered by the Holy Spirit
The Holy Spirit's job is to make us like Jesus and to help us accomplish the mission he sends us on. Therefore, he is the primary discipler and equipper of people. (We'll look at this more next week.)

Gospel saturated
The gospel must permeate the discipling environment. As the gospel seeps into every crack and crevice of our lives, we walk more and more in submission to Jesus, for our good and his glory.

Community influenced
Much of our learning, and growth takes place in community as we serve and experience life together. Without this accountability, most people are likely to keep significant areas of their lives hidden and in sin.

Service oriented
Jesus was consistently serving those in great need. He regularly exposed the disciples to different kinds of people, in different kinds of places, with different kinds of needs. Character qualities like love, compassion, sacrifice, and generosity are more likely to be integrated into our lives as we serve others.

Holistic
Discipleship involves caring for the whole life of a person. Every area of our life needs the gospel, not just the "spiritual" areas like Bible study, prayer, etc. Our time, job, money, relationships, body, etc. must all be shaped from a gospel perspective.

Becoming an apprentice

Frequent and long-term
Jesus spent an incredible amount of time
together with his disciples. Discipleship is
not fast. It takes a lot of time, commitment,
and sacrifice. A discipleship community is
together frequently and cares for each other
over the long-term.

Individually tailored
We see Jesus spending a great deal of time with
the disciples as a group, as well as speaking
specifically into their lives individually.
Discipleship must include a personal focus
as well; knowing each person in a community
has different needs, problems, passions and
spiritual gifts.

Questions:
It was Jesus' plan that his disciples would
be the foundation for the multiplication of
his Church. Part of being a disciple of Jesus
is making more disciples of Jesus.

Since multiplication is a normal part of a
healthy apprenticeship environment, take
some time to evaluate your own community.
What things are you already doing that
help create good environments for the
"apprenticeship" of others? What are the
areas your community could work to grow
in? What are some unique assets (skills,
abilities, networks, key relationships) that
already exist within your community?

7

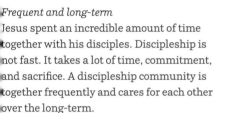

NEXT WEEK...

Ready for an adventure? Make plans to host a party next week.
Invite your sojourner friends.

Starting to think about actively making disciples can seem daunting at first. "Will I need to go out and start recruiting my friends and neighbors in unnatural and awkward ways?"

Remember, you are always in "discipleship mode". You are both being discipled and discipling others all the time, that is what a life of apprenticeship in the Kingdom is like.

Think about the friends, family and acquaintances you already have today. Many of these people are quite possibly sojourners God has brought into your life. Instead of thinking about how you have to "preach" to these people, think about the most natural ways, as a group, you can begin to enter into their story and share God's story with them.

Now think back through the Rhythms (know the story, listen, celebrate, bless, eat, recreate) and ask God to begin to show you how to intentionally integrate your life into the rhythms of these sojourners. This is not an individual effort—you are part of a family of missionary servants!

A COMMON PATTERN

OF NON-CHRISTIAN FRIENDS

LENGTH OF TIME
AS A CHRISTIAN

How can you begin to "share" your friends, family, and acquaintances with others in your community more intentionally?

How are you going to begin their "apprenticeship" through the normal rhythms of everyday life together?

How will you begin to show them the Gospel and invite them to "walk in the ways" of Jesus? (Remember, this is a group endeavor that takes time.)

7

Heroes Of The Faith

As you look for examples to follow in your own apprenticeship of Christ, look at the examples of faith provided in the book of Hebrews.

Now faith is being sure of what we hope for and certain of what we do not see. This is what the ancients were commended for.

By faith we understand that the universe was formed at God's command, so that what is seen was not made out of what was visible.

By faith **Abel** offered God a better sacrifice than Cain did. By faith he was commended as a righteous man, when God spoke well of his offerings. And by faith he still speaks, even though he is dead.

By faith **Enoch** was taken from this life, so that he did not experience death; he could not be found, because God had taken him away. For before he was taken, he was commended as one who pleased God. And without faith it is impossible to please God, because anyone who comes to him must believe that he exists and that he rewards those who earnestly seek him.

By faith **Noah**, when warned about things not yet seen, in holy fear built an ark to save his family. By his faith he condemned the world and became heir of the righteousness that comes by faith.

By faith **Abraham**, when called to go to a place he would later receive as his inheritance, obeyed and went, even though he did not know where he was going. By faith he made his home in the promised land like a stranger in a foreign country; he lived in tents, as did Isaac and Jacob, who were heirs with him of the same promise. For he was looking forward to the city with foundations, whose architect and builder is God.

By faith **Abraham**, even though he was past age—and Sarah herself was barren—was enabled to become a father because he considered him faithful who had made the promise. And so from this one man, and he as good as dead, came descendants as numerous as the stars in the sky and as countless as the sand on the seashore.

All these people were still living by faith when they died. They did not receive the things promised; they only saw them and welcomed them from a distance. And they admitted that they were aliens and strangers on earth. People who say such things show that they are looking for a country of their own. If they had been thinking of the country they had left, they would have had opportunity to return. Instead, they were longing for a better country—a heavenly one. Therefore God is not ashamed to be called their God, for he has prepared a city for them.

By faith **Abraham**, when God tested him, offered Isaac as a sacrifice. He who had received the promises was about to sacrifice his one and only son, even though God had said to him, "It is through Isaac that your offspring will be reckoned." Abraham reasoned that God could raise the dead, and figuratively speaking, he did receive Isaac back from death.

By faith **Isaac** blessed Jacob and Esau in regard to their future.

By faith **Jacob**, when he was dying, blessed each of Joseph's sons, and worshiped as he leaned on the top of his staff.

By faith **Joseph**, when his end was near, spoke about the exodus of the Israelites from Egypt and gave instructions about his bones.

By faith **Moses' parents** hid him for three months after he was born, because they saw he was no ordinary child, and they were not afraid of the king's edict.

By faith **Moses**, when he had grown up, refused to be known as the son of Pharaoh's daughter. He chose to be mistreated along with the people of God rather than to enjoy the pleasures of sin for a short time. He regarded disgrace for the sake of Christ as of greater value than the treasures of Egypt, because he was looking ahead to his reward. By faith he left Egypt, not fearing the king's anger; he persevered because he saw him who is invisible. By faith he kept the Passover and the sprinkling of blood, so that the destroyer of the firstborn would not touch the firstborn of Israel.

By faith **the people** passed through the Red Sea as on dry land; but when the Egyptians tried to do so, they were drowned.

By faith the walls of Jericho fell, after the people had marched around them for seven days.

By faith **the prostitute Rahab**, because she welcomed the spies, was not killed with those who were disobedient.

And what more shall I say? I do not have time to tell about **Gideon**, **Barak**, **Samson**, **Jephthah**, **David**, **Samuel** and **the prophets**, who through faith conquered kingdoms, administered justice, and gained what was promised; who shut the mouths of lions, quenched the fury of the flames, and escaped the edge of the sword; whose weakness was turned to strength; and who became powerful in battle and routed foreign armies. Women received back their dead, raised to life again. Others were tortured and refused to be released, so that they might gain a better resurrection. Some faced jeers and flogging, while still others were chained and put in prison. They were stoned; they were sawed in two; they were put to death by the sword. They went about in sheepskins and goatskins, destitute, persecuted and mistreated — the world was not worthy of them. They wandered in deserts and mountains, and in caves and holes in the ground.

These were all commended for their faith, yet none of them received what had been promised. God had planned something better for us so that only together with us would they be made perfect.

[*Hebrews 11*]

THE INTUITIVE LIFE

100% ORGANIC

So, here we are at the end of our eight weeks together. We'd guess that by now you are beginning to understand the high calling and responsibility of being a missional Christian and influencing people around you incarnationally. But you may also have become aware of the many barriers to living this way, especially as they increase our own susceptibility to consumerism, materialism, and individualism. Even more, we have the normal obstacles of life: work, health, family, finances, global concerns, pressures, problems, and just plain fatigue.

We hope that if you remember anything about this process, you'll focus on the fact that incarnational community can happen anywhere. If you perceive it as one more program you need to add to your already complicated life, you'll never make it.

But if you understand this as something more fundamental, that is, something central to who you are—part of your identity in Christ—then you may be surprised at what God can do in your life. What we're talking about is really personal transformation. It is the process of developing new habits of life and new concepts of what it means to be "on mission." We have a special name for this process: the Intuitive Life.

Intuition is the ability to sense or know without conscious reasoning. Learning to live intuitively is really about learning to live life in faith led and guided by the Holy Spirit. Life rarely happens in steps, programs, or logical sequences. In fact, most of the time, it just happens. Developing an intuitive, incarnational lifestyle is a process and depends on our willingness to listen and respond to God's direction. For it to emerge, we must learn to trust God and lean on faith, being certain that his Holy Spirit is faithfully working in and through us.

8

Is your heart ready to take ownership of Christ's call to mission?

If not, what are you still struggling with?

What are the key lightbulbs that have lit up in your heart and head during the eight weeks of this study?

What areas of transformation have you begun to experience?

now listen, you who say, today or tomorrow we will go to this or that city, spend a year there, carry on business and make money. why, you do not even know what will happen tomorrow.

what is your life? you are a mist that appears for a little while and then vanishes.

8

instead, you ought to say,
if it is the lord's will, we will live
and do this or that.

[james 4:13-17]

Think of a title that describes the season of life you're in right now and write it below. Does that title mostly represent a drama, a comedy, or an action adventure to you at this point? How so?

What are some of the unique opportunities of this season?

What are some limitations of this season?

Describe some plans you've made in the past that assumed too much about your future. How did the plans turn out?

8

Obviously, you can't just decide to be "intuitive" and led by the Spirit. It's something you grow into over time and learn to tune your heart and ear to. Often the things we feel weakest in, or most afraid of, are the very things the Spirit is waiting to do in and through us!

Do a quick study of what Jesus and Paul have to say about the role and work of the Spirit in our lives.

What do you learn about the work of the Holy Spirit from each of these verses?

John 14:15-20
John 14:26
John 15:26
John 16:7-15
Romans 8:5-14
1 Corinthians 2:10-14
Galatians 5:16-26

MAY THE GOD OF HOPE FILL
YOU WITH ALL JOY AND PEACE
AS YOU TRUST IN HIM, SO
THAT YOU MAY OVERFLOW WITH
HOPE BY THE POWER OF THE HOLY
SPIRIT.

I MYSELF AM CONVINCED, MY BROTHERS
AND SISTERS, THAT YOU YOURSELVES ARE
FULL OF GOODNESS, FILLED WITH KNOWLEDGE AND
COMPETENT TO INSTRUCT ONE ANOTHER

THEREFORE I GLORY IN CHRIST JESUS IN MY SERVICE TO
GOD...THROUGH THE POWER OF THE SPIRIT OF GOD.

[ROMANS 15: 13-14; 17,19]

8

The Pressure is Off!
When you read through the passages on the previous page, you probably noticed some of the things the Holy Spirit does in and through us...

He helps, reminds, convicts, teaches, leads, empowers, counsels, reveals...

Often, these are the very same things we think WE are supposed to be working hard at as Christians or leaders in our church. The pressure is off! This is the work of the Spirit now living inside of you. This is a part of this new "intuitive life".

How does this Kingdom reality change the way you might respond to unique or surprising circumstances?

How can you become a better "listener" to the voice of the Holy Spirit?

Will anything else in your life need to have the volume turned down in order to better hear the Spirit?

What areas of your life do you need to let the Spirit lead and empower you? (Think about what most wears you out or brings about stress.)

8

The most simple adjustment we can make to create room for a spontaneous, intuitive life is to cut out the things we don't need to do, opening up time to listen to God's Spirit (remember, listening is one of our Rhythms.) It's so easy to get caught in patterns of saying "yes" to everything. Then, when God wants to use us, we either don't hear him or we're too busy or exhausted to respond.

Cleaning out the clutter in our lives is especially difficult when *good* things are taking up our time. The intuitive life—knowing what to keep and what to get rid of—requires that we listen carefully to God as he guides us in creating more space in the margins of our lives.

8

What is the Holy Spirit asking you to say "NO" to in order to be more available and engaged in incarnational, missional living?

What is the Holy Spirit asking you to say "YES" to in order to further live out your life as part of God's family of missionary servants?

Party time! Make sure a few people stay to help clean up afterwards.

8

Let's make it real.

Here are your instructions...

throw a party.
invite some sojourners.

[Read 4.4 again for some tips on hospitality.]

NEXT WEEK...

Wow. That was fast! Here we are at the end of the 8 weeks.
Make plans to get together next week to figure out what's next.

On the evening of that first day of the week, when the disciples were together, with the doors locked for fear of the Jews, Jesus came and stood among them and said, Peace be with you! After he said this, he showed them his hands and side. The disciples were overjoyed when they saw the Lord.

Again Jesus said, Peace be with you! As the Father has sent me, I am sending you. And with that he breathed on them and said, Receive the Holy Spirit.

(John 20:19-22)

Even though we've focused on incarnational community, the overarching reality is that you are a part of God's Church worldwide. For some of you, your incarnational community will be your local church. For others, your incarnational community will be one community within a large organized church body.

If you are part of an existing church but aren't quite sure how to live in both worlds, we would say: relax. Realize that you are modeling and living out a missional expression of that church. Recognize that everyone is not at the same place in his or her spiritual journey. Learn to enjoy your freedom without expecting everyone else to follow.

The good news is that if the story of your community is strong, eventually a grassroots missional movement can spread to others in the larger church. In the meantime, realize that people will always be watching and learning from your journey. We suggest that you try not to overthink the issue of church. Just get on mission, and pray for those that are less eager to embrace change.

8

We would like to leave you with one of the great scenes in scripture...the day that Christ reappeared to his disciples after his crucifixion. At the time, they were confused, distraught, and not very confident about God's work in their lives. To them, Jesus uttered this call: "As the Father has sent me, I am sending you."

As this study comes to a close, consider this same call for your own life.

If you are part of a traditional church, today would be a good time to write your pastor a note or email of thanks and encouragement for all he does in caring for the fearful, the complacent, the distracted, and all the rest of the diverse body of Christ.

If you're not part of a church, write a note of thanks to the people that have significantly influenced your spiritual journey.

8

Consider: God has always wanted a family that would live in such a way that they would show the world what he is truly like. As Christians, we are the fulfillment of God's eternal plan. We now have God's own Spirit living inside of us–the same power that raised Christ from the dead. Rest in that power!

THE KINGDOM OF HEAVEN IS LIKE TREASURE HIDDEN IN A FIELD. WHEN A MAN FOUND IT, HE HID IT AGAIN, AND THEN IN HIS JOY WENT AND SOLD ALL HE HAD AND BOUGHT THAT FIELD.

AGAIN, THE KINGDOM OF HEAVEN IS LIKE A MERCHANT LOOKING FOR FINE PEARLS. WHEN HE FOUND ONE OF GREAT VALUE, HE WENT AWAY AND SOLD EVERYTHING HE HAD AND BOUGHT IT.

[MATTHEW 13:44-45]

100% SOLD

EPILOGUE

Congratulations!

You've reached the end of the primer! By now you should have learned a lot about what it means to live a missional life in the context of incarnational community. But the biggest question you have right now is probably this: WHAT'S NEXT?

The following process might help you sort out where your community is headed...

DEBRIEF

The way Jesus made disciples was to ask them to "do" something that disoriented or challenged them, and then he debriefed, taught, and helped them process what they were learning. As you may now recognize, the primers are intended to do the same thing. Success is not what you did with the 8 weeks, but what you learned about yourself and your community through this.

These final questions are the most important for you to consider and will fuel the future of what following Jesus will be like for you. Please take the time to consider these questions.

Personal Reflection

What did you learn about yourself during this process? Where did you see growth happen in your life?

What areas of spiritual or practical apathy were exposed?

For you to live a life of intentionally missional, personally incarnational community, what will be the biggest hurdles you personally have to deal with?

Community Reflection

Whether you went through the primer with your existing small group or a handful of new friends, it's now time to decide *with whom* and *when* your journey of incarnational community will continue. Are the people you traveled through the primer with the people you now feel called to go on mission with?

As you consider who, try to choose people who are close in proximity, committed to community, and with whom you share personal synergy. In other words, you like them and can see doing mission with them.

The next question is how will you formalize the next period of missional community with them? As you plan, there are a few things to consider...

Timing: When will we start?

Rhythms: What will we commit to doing on a consistent basis? (serving, time in scripture, prayer, recreational time, time with our unchurched friends, blessing others, etc) Choose rhythms that make sense to your personally, and also those you hope to influence toward Christ.

Frequency of rhythms: How often will you meet and for what purposes?

Take notes on your thoughts and the things the community agrees on.

A FINAL THOUGHT FROM HUGH
Although I don't know your name or face, I want you to know that I wish we could be friends.

As I write this, I'm sitting in a sushi bar in the Portland airport. I flew in late last night, and due to bad weather, I got stranded for a while. I talked to one young man who was flying in to check out some colleges. I asked him why he was thinking of moving to the Northwest, and he said, "Just trying to get away from my family."

A few minutes later, I heard a man behind me berating the young server for messing up his hamburger order. He was relentless and did his best to humiliate her in front of everyone. I pictured this dear girl as my 15-year-old daughter and later grabbed her hand as she went to take my empty glass. She

was shocked that I wouldn't let go, and while looking into her eyes, I said, "You're doing a great job. Forget about that knucklehead." She teared up and gave me heartfelt, "Thank you, sir." I left her a $20 tip on my $5 appetizer and headed to the hotel at 2:00 am.

While putting the key card into my room door, I saw a young twenty-something gal leaving the room next to me. It was obvious that she was a prostitute. She walked quickly past me, keeping her head down.

The next morning, I went to speak to some denominational leaders about the impending death of many of their churches, and maybe their entire denominational movement. They spoke candidly of the silly fights their pastors and parishioners get into; a host of pathetic misuses of funding and programs; and failed attempts to revive the hearts of their people.

Now, as I have a few hours to think about you before I head back to Denver, I'm moved with emotion about how open and desperate this world is to know a good friend like you. I think about how God changed the world with just a handful of faithful followers, and I love the thought of us all working diligently to be his hands, his feet, his voice, and his face to this world. I feel grateful that God has overwhelmed me with his invitation to join him and, while I don't know you personally, I feel incredibly honored to extend this invitation to you now.

Please receive this blessing as my prayer for you: To you, my fellow traveler, may God explode your heart with gratefulness for salvation, with anger over injustice, with love for

*the loveless, with selfless hours of service, with
words that bring hope, and homes that bring
warmth. May Christ be in the food you serve;
may he interrupt your schedule with moments
that change the destiny of families; may his
purposes become your purposes; and may the
things that break his heart break yours. May
he supply to you all that is needed to live large
in the Kingdom that is now and yet to come,
and may we someday meet along a heavenly
riverbank and meet each other's friends that
now know the King of Glory because of you.*

See you on the other side...the better side!

Peace out,
Hugh

FOR ADDITIONAL HELP
Although it's up to you and your community
to chart your own incarnational way of life,
we want to make sure you know where to
find friends, and additional help.

For deeper learning on missional
and incarnational community, visit
missiopublishing.com (click on resources and
media).

Resources from Missio Publishing

The Tangible Kingdom Primer

The *Tangible Kingdom Primer* is designed to help Christians, churches, and small groups get on the pathway of spiritual formation and missional engagement. This primer creates opportunities to experience authentic missional community step-by-step. It leads participants on a challenging 8-week journey toward an incarnational lifestyle and moves far beyond the typical small group experience. The *Tangible Kingdom Primer* is a great starting point when trying to transition existing small groups toward more incarnational and missional rhythms.

The Gospel Primer

Many in our churches have spent years listening to sermons, studying theology and reading the Word of God, yet still feel intimidated or unable to naturally express the good news of the Gospel into normal life, conversations, and circumstances.

In community, over 8 weeks, the *Gospel Primer* will help you creatively learn: What is the Gospel? We'll look at the Story of God that illustrates the gospel throughout all of scripture. You'll learn how to form and tell your personal 'My Gospel Story' in a natural, yet powerful way. We'll also look at how the Gospel has actually given us a new identity in Christ and how to live out the truth of this gospel identity in the normal rhythms of everyday life. We know of no other resource that can help you gain such a useable understanding and practice of the Gospel in such a short period of time.

The Justice Primer

Everyone's talking about social action and justice in the world. And for the first time in a long while, the Western church is looking for something designed to collectively point people outward and to give them a platform to do so together in community.

The ch*Justice Primer* is designed to be your guide on the journey of "learning to do right." It leads participants on a practical 8-week journey to put mission back into your small group or faith community. It's designed to help existing groups and churches begin or continue their journey toward being missional. If you desire to relearn the posture required to become missionaries in your context, and to equip others to engage culture through engaging the needs around them, the *Justice Primer* is your pilot.

Additional Resources For Your Journey

In addition to our primer series, we recommend these other books from Missio Publishing and our authors.

The Permanent Revolution Playbook

There is clear guidance from Scripture itself as to how the church can be the fullness of Christ in the world. A vital part of the answer to a renewed ministry matching the challenges we face, is found in Eph.4:1-16. The **Permanent Revolution Playbook** by Alan Hirsch and Tim Catchim is designed to introduce individual disciples or teams to their own, Jesus-given, vocational profile.

BIVO: A Modern-Day Guide for Bi-Vocational Saints

The Gospel came to us through fully paid, barely paid, and mostly non-paid saints. The future of Kingdom life and ministry depends on God's people to finding creative pathways for leveraging all of life into one calling. **BiVO** by Hugh Halter is a story and a framework to help you find this leverage point whether you are a marketplace leader or ministry leader.

Bigger Gospel: Learning To Speak, Live and Enjoy the Good News in Every Area of Life

Have you wished you could share your Christian faith with others in a natural way without feeling awkward or preachy? Have you ever longed for a faith that touched down more than just Sunday-to-Sunday leading up to one long afterlife?

Bigger Gospel will help you develop the confidence and grace to speak the truth in love—first to your self—and then with others in a way that is truly good news. Evangelism will no longer be a weird or stressful sales pitch and your discipleship and conversations will be supercharged with good news.

Missio Publishing is committed to resourcing the church with practical tools to help it engage more effectively in missional and incarnational ministry. To purchase the Primers and other resources, along with bulk discounts for churches, visit **missiopublishing.com**